THE VERY BEST GROUP GAMES EVER PLAYED

table of contents

DEDICATION

This book is dedicated to my parents, Harold and Grace Kinziger, for their willingness to sacrifice their own dreams in order that my brothers, sisters and I achieve ours. Thank you, Mom and Dad, for teaching self determination, for providing me with self-confidence and for believing in the value of education. Thank you most of all for allowing me to have fun and to enjoy life to its fullest. I love you.

ACKNOWLEDGMENTS

While it is impossible to thank everyone who in some way contributed to this collection of the 100 very best group games ever played, I would like to express my sincere gratitude and appreciation to all of the students and participants who volunteered to play and help refine the material presented in this book. Thanks for expressing confidence, interest, and your enthusiasm and for laughing a lot.

I am particularly indebted to my good friend, Tim Lorman, for his donation of time, talent, encouragement and laughter throughout the years. I also need to thank my daughters for editing, DJ Werlau for initial art work and to Nick Cain for the creative and exhaustive update to the new editions. Most of all, I want to thank all of the authors of the many "game" books that I have examined since my interest in play that started in graduate school after I returned from a tour of duty during the Viet Nam conflict. Your material stimulated an excitement in me that never seemed to die.

Finally, I must acknowledge my beautiful, bright, and "guinea pig" daughters Khea, Kasey and Kody for their patience, support and love throughout the years as well as supplying me with a good dose of reality checks as we experimented and played many of the activities. Thanks for all of the playful and powerful memories we have shared.

DISCLAIMER

Reasonable risk-taking is part of life. Games and activities should not be undertaken without the supervision of a leader/s that understand and practice effective leading techniques as suggested in this book. When special equipment is used, it is imperative that the leader/s make sure that the gear is safe and in operational shape. The leader/s of the activities and games in this book assume all risk and liability for the interpretation and implementation of the games for the groups. No book or leading guide can substitute for experience and education. It is also highly recommended that activities are lead with a "challenge by choice" philosophy. Allowing participants to communicate their comfort levels is always better than mandatory participation. Good luck, play safe, stay healthy and active and most important, have fun!

WHY THIS BOOK

Please Note: The large majority of this book used to be called, KING FROG, hence the frog graphics. This book has been edited and more professionally prepared for the audience that will be using the contents.

Finally, a game leader's "dream" book that is thorough and yet succinctly written that combines group games that actually have been played and that participants immensely enjoy. Here in one book are all of the elements for effectively leading and participating in group games that are fun, require little or moderate equipment, that range from high to low energy and that can be played with players from all ages. The unique and consistent game template with a game on each page is easy to follow and results with leaders and players getting the most out of the activities.

If you ever wanted to own just one book.....one game book.... this is it! Inside you will find the 100 very best group games ever played along with key terminology, play statements, effective teaching techniques, It Power guidelines, methods to select teams, learning theory, guidelines for processing the games, tournament information, and a creative game matrix with nearly 3,000,000 different combinations of games.

Playing games can be lots of fun. Leading games can be quite rewarding. The information in this book provides an opportunity to maximize both the fun and effectiveness of leading play activities.

Every game in this book has been played and re-played, analyzed and tweaked and written from the heart by an author who loves to have fun, laugh and to see others caught up in the enjoyment of play.

Games are not just frivolous or about playing ..... people tend to play the way they live their lives. We can learn a lot about players when games are a "tool" to observe human behavior. Effective leading and leaders who ask the "good" questions can make the play experience more powerful.

The "template" format of the book is unique and treats each game as a serious endeavor. Nearly all games include the same "ingredients", what a great idea to prepare them with consistency. Variations and safety considerations to each game create new and fun possibilities.

Games can be used for many, many purposes. So why not be realistic and include tag, guessing, competitive, collective score, team building, problem solving, relay and name games? Why not let the leaders and the people who buy the book decide how they will use the material?

The appendices and all of the support material make leading these games much easier and more fun for all involved.

The Creative Game and Play Matrix is a special addition. In the past, hundreds of games have been created from the matrix and here is my observation: Children tend to create games where 1) all children play ... no one has to wait in line; 2) children rarely eliminate players from the game as the game continues, and 3) children seldom create games that require hitting. Those seem to be adult concepts!

A PARABLE

In the beginning, there weren't just one or two players. There were a whole bunch of us! Our "game leader" wanted us to have a lot of fun and said you can't really have fun unless there's a whole gang of you. So we all went to a playground and were told to enjoy. At first we did have fun just like expected. We played all of the time! We rolled down hills, climbed in the trees, ran in the meadows, hid in the forest and just acted silly. We sure laughed a lot!

Then one day this game leader told us we weren't really having fun because we weren't keeping score. Back then, we didn't know what score was. And when that shady character explained score to all of us, we still couldn't see the fun in that. Then we were told that a shiny apple should be given to the person who was best at playing and we'd never know who was best unless we kept score. We could all see the fun in that. We were all sure we were best.

It was different after that. We yelled a lot. We swore. We had to make up new scoring rules for most of the games we played. By the time the game leader found out about our new fun, we were spending almost all of our time working out the score. We were told we couldn't use the playground anymore because we weren't having any fun. We said we were having lots of fun and we were. There was no need to get so upset. We were kicked out of the playground and told we couldn't come back until we stopped keeping score and stopped trying to beat each other. To rub it in, we were told that the games in our future would be too difficult to play alone and that we would have to learn to play together and not always against each other.

Well..., we decided to do something about our fate. We decided to play games where winning wasn't the only way to play. We wanted to have fun again. We didn't care who was best anymore. We just wanted to play. By luck one day, we met a new game leader. He told us about effective game teaching and playing techniques. He told us about "It Power". We learned that almost every game we could play involved catching or tagging. Our challenge would be to use our new knowledge to make our games exciting and more fun. We wanted more proof. Group juggling was one game that we were having little fun with. It seemed that no one could catch and that the game was boring. The leader told us to reduce the size of the play field and to change the position of the players so they were closer together. He organized us into a circle and gave us brief instructions. The game was also carefully demon-

strated to us. We were told that it was OK to change the rules for the players in the game. We started playing slowly. The equipment was ready for us to play with. Questions were encouraged. We got

absorbed in the game. Some of the players even laughed out loud.
Then it happened. The game became less fun. It was too easy. What could we do? We decided to increase the number of throwers by adding more equipment. The game became fun again! But soon it happened again. It was too easy. We tried to remember what the new leader had taught us. We decided to all take five steps backward to change our positions. We decided to change our mode of locomotion from standing still to moving in a clockwise circle. We also threw the objects instead of handing them to each other. What a difference!

We then remembered that we should stop a game at a high point when the game flow is at its peak. Was it only a coincidence that we were having so much fun? We decided to try another game, this time a tag game. Would our new techniques work? We decided to play Freeze Tag. We selected an IT. The play area was defined and instructions were given. At a given starting signal, the game began. The game was a disaster. The IT could not freeze everyone fast enough and became exhausted. We stopped play. What could we do? We picked a different IT. We decided to change the starting signal and the starting position of the IT. The game was still a disaster! Again play was stopped. We decided to add more ITS. We also decided to reduce the size of the play field.
Our changes made a remarkable difference. Freeze tag became a game of skill and challenge. Our attitude toward the playing of games had changed. We had discovered effective game teaching and IT POWER. We realized that we didn't need to know hundreds of games to have fun. It was apparent that score wasn't as important as we were made to believe. We understood the spirit of the game. We were having fun just playing.
What we really discovered was that life on a playground was only one place to have fun. We can laugh, be creative and enjoy the companionship of others wherever we choose. We are very grateful and look forward to sharing our wonderful knowledge with you as our new game leader did with us. Our hope is that you too will laugh more and play more and someday share the spirit of IT POWER and effective game teaching with others. Let's make wherever we play as fun and rewarding as possible!

READ THIS FIRST

I started writing The Very Best Group Games Ever Played and Much More while a graduate Ph. D. student in New Mexico in 1990. I had been introduced to the "New Games" movement as a Teaching Assistant while pursuing a MS degree in recreation at Wisconsin-Lacrosse in 1978. I have been leading and playing games and conducting workshops for more than thirty years. These games and the material in this book may serve as a legacy and will answer two questions that have been asked of me thousands of times, "Is there a place where your games are written down?" And.... "How can I access them?" And the answer is...... "Keep reading"!

PREFACE

Games and play are critical and indispensable activities. They are important to normal development. Play has the power to unite the conscious and the non-conscious. It can be simultaneously reflective and frivolous. It can be silly and serious. Play can restructure our lives by establishing simple yet powerful rules that change relationships and interactions. Play can serve as a tool to help us understand how we behave and act in the "real" world.

Games and play form the basis for experiencing fun, success, happiness and growth. Play, therefore, is a unique human activity which should not be measured in terms of how individuals perform against each other, but rather in a group process. Utilizing effective techniques when leading a series of games so an individual can experience, learn, and develop positive social attitudes and physical skills is essential. Play still needs to be fun. It needs more spontaneity and less repetition. Children and adults can benefit from the activity found in cooperative play and games where the process of play is more important than the outcome. The leader or teacher must be aware and use effective techniques when leading games and team building activities so participants can experience, learn, and develop positive social attitudes and physical skills.

Much of activity today focuses on the improvement of physical fitness and the development of competitive skills, but not on the development of creative play or team building skills. Equally important is an emphasis on the process and processing of play versus the emphasis on outcome. Physical exercise is a necessary component to the physical and mental development of a child and in today's world may also be crucial for a healthy active lifestyle for adults. Play can function like sleep: it recharges us and helps us reorganize our outlooks more positively. Play is for anyone and everyone, not just for those who are best at play. Skill should not be the pre-requisite to play... wanting to play should be! Effective game and activity leaders can facilitate activity so the participant can experience, learn and develop positive social, psychological and physical skills.

TAG GAMES

ALLIGATOR
BLOB
BROKEN SPOKE
CAT AND MOUSE
CATCH DRAGON'S TAIL
ELBOW TAG
FREEZE TAG
GIANTS, WIZARDS ELVES
GO TAG
HEADS AND TAILS TAG
HOSPITAL TAG
HUG TAG
LEMONADE
NEEDLE & THREAD TAG
OCTOPUS
PAIRS & PAIRS SQUARED
QUEEN BEE TAG
SHARK
SIDE-BY-SIDE TAG
SNAKE PIT
SWAT
STOMP AND POP
TRIANGLE TAG
WORLD'S FASTEST TAG

GUESSING GAMES

COLANDER GAME
ELEPHANT/TREE/MONKEY FA-
MOUS PEOPLE GAME
FANTASY GO-AROUND
FISH GOBBLER
IMPULSE
KILLER
PRUI
LEMONADE
MIME RHYMES
SCARE BEAR
TWO TRUTHS AND A LIE
UP JENKINS
WHAT AND WHERE
WHO'S THERE?
WHO STARTED THE STAMPEDE
ZEN COUNTDOWN

RELAY GAMES

AIRPLANE RELAY
COOKIE MACHINE
FOUR SQUARE RELAY
HOWDY, NEIGHBOR
JACK BE NIMBLE RELAY
LAUGHING LOGS

SKIN THE SNAKE
WHEEL AND SPOKES

NAME GAMES

BUMPITY-BUMP-BUMP-BUMP
DO YOU KNOW YOUR NEIGHBOR
FANTASY GO-AROUND
FIRE ON THE MOUNTAIN
GROWTH CIRCLES
HUSTLE BUSTLE
NAME BY NAME
PEOPLE TO PEOPLE
SOUND AND FURY
TWO TRUTHS AND A LIE
WHO'S THERE?

COMPETITIVE GAMES

AH-SO-KO
AIRPLANE RELAY
ALL CATCH AND UP CHUCK
AROUND AND AROUND
BALLOON FRENZY
KINZI
BRITISH BULLDOG
BUG RACING
BUMPER BALL
CATCH THE DRAGON'S TAIL
DANCING DRACULA
DHO, DHO, DHO!
FAMOUS PEOPLE GAME FOUR
SQUARE RELAY
GIANTS, WIZARDS & ELVES
GO TAG
NOODLE FACE OFF
IMPULSE
JACK BE NIMBLE RELAY
KILLER
NEEDLE AND THREAD TAG
NEW" MUSICAL CHAIRS
OCTOPUS
QUICK LINE-UP
ROCK/PAPER/SCISSORS RELAY
SKIN THE SNAKE
STAND OFF
STOMP AND POP
SWAT
TAFFY PULL
TRIANGLE TAG
UP JENKINS
WAVE
WHEEL AND SPOKES
WHO'S THERE?
WINK

WORLD'S FASTEST TAG GAME

COLLECTIVE SCORE

ALL CATCH AND UP CHUCK
BARNYARD
DANCING DRACULA
FREEZE TAG
GROUP JUGGLING
GROUP JUMP ROPE
NURSERY RHYME GAME
POPSICLE PUSH-UPS
ROCK/PAPER/SCISSORS
SINGIN' IN THE SUN
TREE BALL

PROBLEM SOLVING GAMES

AH-SO-KO
BIG WIND BLOWS
BIRTHDAY LINE-UP
BUMPER BALL
DOODLES
FAMOUS PEOPLE GAME
FENCE
FLIPPITY FLIP
KING FROG
HUMAN KNOTS
LAP SIT
LEMONADE
MIME RHYMES
NAME BY NAME
NUMBER TO NUMBER
ONBOARD
POPCORN
POPSICLE PUSH-UPS
PRUI
PYRAMIDS
QUICK LINE-UP
RACCOON CIRCLES
ROCK/PAPER/SCISSORS
ROCK/PAPER/SCISSORS RELAY
SCARE BEAR
SHERPA WALK
TANDEM JUGGLING
TINY TEACHINGS
TOUCH AND GO
TRAFFIC JAM

7

game table

game table

Game	Level	Game	Level
Needle and Thread Tag	65	Airplane Relay	92
Laughing Logs	66	Kinzi	93
Popsicle Push-Ups	67	Group Jump Rope	94
Impulse	68	Rock, Paper, Scissors Relay	95
People to People	69	Stomp and Pop	96
Queen Bee Tag	70	Wink	97
Swat	71	Hug Tag	98
Lemonade	72	Heads and Tails Tag	99
Skin the Snake	73	Hospital Tag	100
Snake Pit	74	Around and Around	101
Alligator	75	Octopus	102
Big Wind Blows	76	Blob	103
Cat and Mouse	77	Broken Spoke	104
Shark	78	Wheel and Spokes	105
Touch and Go	79	Triangle Tag	108
Four Square Relay	80	Go Tag	109
Giants, Wizards, and Elves	81	World's Fastest Tag Game	110
Do You Know Your Neighbor	82	Catch the Dragons Tail	111
Quick Line-Up	83	Freeze Tag	112
Wave	84	Elbow Tag	113
Who Started the Stampede	85	Pairs and Pairs Squared	114
Fire on the Mountain	86	Side by Side tag	115
Cookie Machine	87	British Bulldog	116
Sound and Fury	90	Dho, Dho, Dho!	117
Stand Off	91	Taffy Pull	

9

easy

energy level

Quick Description

Famous People Game- guessing and competitive game naming famous people for 3-50 people with groups of 2-5 players for middle school to adults. (Score sheets for each team)

Mime Rhymes- a quiet small group guessing game involving miming out words for 4-8 players for elementary to adults. (Mime game list)

Zen Countdown- a great game to end a game session that requires players to work together to accomplish a goal for 4-10 players for middle school to adults. (No equipment)

Rock Paper Scissors- a small group challenge using the rock/paper/scissors signs for 4-28 players with group size at four for middle school to adults. (No equipment)

Nursery Rhyme Game- a small group singing game that rotates between groups for 5-40 players with groups of 5-8 players for all ages. (Nursery game list)

Doodles- a problem solving game that helps players get to know each other for 12-30 players for middle school to adults. (Doodle sheets for each player)

Fantasy Go-Around- a fun game involving guessing players fantasies for 5-12 players for high school to adults. (Fantasy sheet for each player)

Two Truths and a Lie- a special type of sharing and guessing game that helps players get to know each other for 6-12 players for high school to adult. (Sheet of paper per player)

King Frog- a excellent small group game of verbal and repeated actions for 7-12 players for middle school to adults. (No equipment)

Colander Game- a spirited guessing game for 7-12 players for high school to adults. (Colander or large bowl)

Bug Racing- a competitive "environmental" activity for 8, 16 or 32 players for elementary to adults. (Game board, cups with lids)

Human Knots- a team building and problem solving game using rope for 8-12 players for elementary to adults. (Short piece of rope for each player)

Traffic Jam- a small group challenge that requires the group to problem solve a solution for 8-10 players for middle school to adults. (Markers with arrows)

What and Where- a game of continued confusion with conversation going in two directions for 8-20 players for middle school to adults. (One object and one piece of paper)

Barnyard- a creative and fun activity to arrange players into equal groups for 10-60 players of all ages. (No equipment)

Ah-So-Ko- a quick paced action elimination game for 10-30 players for middle school to adults. (No equipment)

Up Jenkins- a combination of a guessing and competitive game where one tam tries to guess who has coins in their hand for 10-20 players for middle school to adults. (Table, chairs and a coin)

Scare Bear- a hilarious group prank type game for 8-40 players for high school to adults. (No equipment)

Birthday Line-Up- a group and individual challenge game for 12-50 players for elementary to adults. (Marker for each player)

Singin' in the Sun- a singing game with various collective gestures for 12-50 players for all ages. (No equipment)

Killer- a guessing game where players attempt to locate the killer before being "killed" for 12-30 players for middle school to adults. (No equipment)

Who's There?- a name guessing game where players "pop up" quickly and yell out names of the person across from them for 12-30 players for high school to adult. (Rope and a blanket)

Howdy Neighbors!- a "crazy" relay and competitive game with partners for 14-40 players for middle school to adults. (No equipment)

Dancing Dracula- a musical tag game for 15-40 players for all ages. (Boundary markers and loud music)

Hustle Bustle- a speed game that assists players to get to know names for 15-50 players for elementary to adults. (No equipment)

Name by Name- a combination name and problem solving game for 15-40 players for elementary to adults. (No equipment)

Prui- a trust and guessing activity where players play most of the game with their eyes closed for 15-30 players for high school to adults. (No equipment)

Bumpity-Bump-Bump-Bump- a quick decision name game for 16-40 players for all ages. (No equipment)

Growth Circles- an excellent name game similar to "speed dating" for 16-30 players for high school to adults. (No equipment)

Popcorn- a highly visible activity that involves bouncing numerous balls or objects out of a circle for 20-30 players for all ages. (Parachute or blanket and numerous foam balls)

Elephant/Palm Tree/Monkey- an action tag and guessing game for 20-40 players for all ages. (No equipment)

Flippity Flip- a group challenge activity that requires problem solving and teamwork for 20-30 players for middle school to adults. (Tarp or large blanket)

Lap Sit- a large group physical challenge with the entire group in a large circle for 25-100 players for elementary to adults. (No equipment)

Competitive Game
Guessing Game
Equipment:
Alphabet game score sheet and pen

famous people game

3-30 Players
Middle School to Adult
Play Area:
Indoor or Outdoor

To Begin

A LEADER will arrange players into groups of three to five per group. Multiple groups are recommended. Groups should distance themselves away from other groups to encourage discussion and brain storming. The LEADER will give each group the "FAMOUS PEOPLE GAME" score sheet (see Appendix B, page 140). There are two columns on the score sheet for letters. The left column is lettered from "A" to "Z". The letters for the second column are determined by the LEADER. There needs to be 26 letters.

Next

The LEADER can select words, phrases, sentences, titles, etc. For example, if the LEADER selected "FAMOUS PEOPLE IN THE WORLD GAME", each team would place those letters in sequential order next to the alphabet letters, A-F, B-A, C-M, D-O, E-U, F-S until the final alphabet letter, Z-E. A time limit is established by the LEADER (10 - 15 minutes). Each group attempts to identify a famous name that starts with the first letter and ends with the last letter in each row.

Setup
X = Players

Third

A FAMOUS NAME can be real or fictional. It can be from history, sports, entertainment, cartoons, movies, books, etc. It cannot be friends or family or classmates (unless they are FAMOUS). Groups cannot use titles (Mr, Mrs, King, Queen, President, etc). Groups can only use first and last names. Groups may identify names in any order that they choose and may skip around. NO names can be added once the LEADER stops the game.

Scoring

Scoring takes time. The LEADER'S decision is final. For example: if the first set of letters was A-L, the LEADER would ask each group if they had a name for A-L. If two or more groups have "Abe Lincoln," 5pts are awarded. If two or more groups have "Abe Lincoln," and one group has "Ann Landers," 10pts are awarded for "Ann Landers" and 5pts for "Abe Lincoln". If only one group has come up with a name, they are awarded 25pts. Scoring continues through the entire alphabet.

12

Game Variations Suggestions

1. If a name has been presented that the LEADER does not recognize, the LEADER may request verification from other groups. If one player from any other group recognizes the name as a FAMOUS NAME, the LEADER grants points.
2. With less skilled groups or players, vowels may be eliminated. Use only consonants for last names.

Team Building
Problem Solving
Equipment:
Mime Rhyme Game List

mime rhymes

4-28 Players
Upper Elementary to Adult
Play Area:
Indoor or Outdoor

To Begin

Arrange the participants into groups. Small groups of four to eight players kneel or sit in a "tight" circle together. The LEADER will have a copy of the Mime Rhyme Game List (See Appendix E - Page 143) and explain how the game is played. The LEADER will supply each group RHYMER with a KEY WORD and the MIME WORD for each game. If there is only one group, the LEADER can be the RHYMER.

Next

One player (the RHYMER) starts the game by receiving the KEY WORD and MIME WORD from the LEADER. The RHYMER verbally tells all of the players in the group the KEY WORD. The key word will rhyme with the word to be guessed by the rest of the players.

Setup

X = Players
O = Leader or Rhymer

Third

The RHYMER starts off by saying, "I have in mind a word that rhymes with ...." The rest of the players attempt to guess the MIME WORD without talking or making a sound. Players must communicate with eye contact and clear actions. If a player thinks they know the MIME WORD, they must raise their hand. The RHYMER will recognize that player by pointing or with a nod of the head.

Continue Play

When the player has been recognized by the RHYMER, the player will act out their guess by using a MIME. The MIME should be acted out for all of the players in the group to see. They can sit, stand or use their body as they see fit. If the wrong word is MIMED, the RHYMER will shake his/her head "NO". Players may guess as often as they want when recognized. When a correct guess is MIMED, the next player in the circle becomes the RHYMER. Action continues until all of the players have had one or two turns.

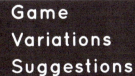

13

Team Building
Guessing Game
Equipment:
None

4-10 Players
Middle School to Adult
Play Area:
Indoor or Outdoor

zen countdown

To Begin

All of the players gather together in the play area. The players form a small, tight cirlce and face toward the center. The LEADER is part of the circle and should be familiar with the game.

Next

The LEADER is responsible for starting the game and is the only one who can begin the countdown. The LEADER beings the countdown by calling out the first number, "20".

Setup

X = Players
O = Leader

Third

Any player may call out the following number (19) and then (18) until the group counts down to "0". However, if two or more players speak at the same time, or if someone calls out the wrong number, the LEADER must start a new countdown beginning again with "20".

Rules

The LEADER may participate in the countdown by calling out other numbers. One player cannot call out more than two numbers in a row. Avoid establishing a pattern, such as simply going around the circle. If it becomes too difficult to complete the countdown, the LEADER can begin with a lower number, such as "15", "10" or ever "5".

Game Variations Suggestions

1. The game requires concentration and teamwork. Avoid a pattern. Players should not point or look directly at a player to encourage that player to call out a number.

2. If the group is struggling, start the count at "5" so that the game ends with group success. This is a great game to end a session of play.

Problem Solving
Collective Score
Equipment:
None

rock paper scissors

4-28 Players
Middle School to Adult
Play Area:
Indoor or Outdoor

To Begin

Players form into groups of four players. Groups scatter thoughout the play area so there is sufficient room to allow movement for the game to be played. One of the players in each group is chosen to be the IT for that group. The IT will lead the action.

Next

There are three hand actions in this game and each group should practice these actions before beginning. To begin, the left hand should be open, palm facing up at the belt line with the little finger close to the body. The right hand starts as a fist, thumb side up. On a 1...2 count from the IT, the fist hits the palm of the open left hand twice (once on "1" and once on "2").

# Setup
X = Players
IT = Group IT

Third

On the third count, the right hand is extended forward and forms one of three signs. The signs are: ROCK, a fist; PAPER, open hand with palm facing down; and SCISSORS, the first two fingers separated and pointing forward, the remaining two fingers and thumb closed into a fist.

Objective

The objective of the game is for all of the players to form the same sign...twice! To do this, the players need to concentrate on the sign they form and the signs formed by other players. Players may not perform the same sign more than twice in a row and players may not verbally communicate by announcing a sign that the group should perform. The IT should keep the pace of the game moving quickly.

15

Game
Variations
Suggestions

1. When a team has accomplished the goal, the players on that team will circle around a team that is still attempting to complete the goal.

2. Select teams of five players (very difficult).
3. Each team should attempt to not perform the same sign at the same time.... twice.

Collective Score
Team Building
Equipment:
Nursery Rhyme List

nursery rhyme game

5-40 Players
Lower Elem. to Adult
Play Area:
Indoor or Outdoor

To Begin

Players form 1 to 8 groups of five to six players per group. Groups arrange themselves close together in a circle (or semi circle) near the LEADER. The LEADER allows each group to review a list of nursery rhymes (See Appendix F - Page 144) from the NURSERY RHYMES LIST. Groups should spend some time with the list selecting nursery rhymes they are familiar with. Time should be alloted for each group to practice the nursery rhymes that they may eventually sing.

Next

The LEADER must know the alphabet and be able to sing it to an established tune. See Appendix G- Page 145) for the music score. The LEADER sings through the first verse of the tune substituting letters of the alphabet for the words of the tune. The LEADER should practice this in advance so he/she is comfortable singing the song. The chorus: + ABCDEFGHIJKLM......

Setup

X = Players
L = Leader

L

Third

After the LEADER solo, the entire group sings the tune again with all of the players participating. (Hint: It is necessary to practice the chorus a few times before the game begins). This is the group "chorus" that is repeated by all the groups throughout the game. The LEADER will then demonstrate a nursery rhyme (Jack and Jill Went Up the Hill) which is sung to the same chorus. The LEADER gives each group a starting number (1st, 2nd, etc.). The game begins with all of the players and the LEADER singing the chorus.

Rules

After the group chorus (A-Z), the first group attempts to sing a nursery rhyme to the same tune as the chorus. When the group is done, all of the players again sing the group chorus. The second group then attempts to sing a different nursery rhyme. Again, all of the players sing the group chorus when the second group is done with their rhyme. The game continues with this sequence and continues to be played even if there are mistakes with a nursery rhyme by a group. Two to five rounds make an good game.

16

Game Variations Suggestions

1. At the conclusion of the game, each group is given a paper and pencil. Each group will then "create" their own "nursery rhyme" to the chorus tune.

When all groups are ready, another round of singing the NURSERY RHYME GAME will begin: chorus first and each groups original verse follows.

Team Building
Problem Solving
Equipment:
Doodle Sheet & Pen

doodles

5-12 Players
Middle School to Adult
Play Area:
Desks or Flat Area

To Begin

Players arrange themselves in a circle with enough distance for private space. The LEADER will be part of the circle. Desks or tables are best. Each player will be given their own DOODLE SHEET and writing utensil by the LEADER. Colored pencils that all players can share is ideal. Each player will complete all four DOODLES in a given time frame (usually 5-7 minutes). A question for each DOODLE is provided at the top of each DOODLE BOX. The LEADER provides no other information. Players should not talk to one another or share ideas at this time.

Next

The LEADER collects all of the DOODLE SHEETS when time is up. All of the DOODLE SHEETS are laid out on a table for all players to view. The LEADER then shares the information about each DOODLE (see DOODLE information below). The LEADER and the players will view and discuss one DOODLE at a time. The LEADER may single out individuals and ask them why they "DOODLED" what they "DOODLED". This is a fun activity to process.

Setup

SEE APPENDIX A Page 139
Doodle Game Sheet

Third

CONFIDENCE: The line in the middle of the block indicates confidence in the world. Items above the line are objects which a player has command over. Items below the line are things which are generally out of a players control.
PERSONAL MOTTO: What a player draws on this sign suggests a personal statement or belief. If positive, a player has a pleasant outlook on life. If the sign is a warning, watch out! If a sign indicates direction, a player is ready for a change in their life.

Objective

HOME: If a player draws within the box, their interests are within the home. If they draw outside the box, their interests are outside the home. Home symbols such as fireplace, windows, and doors indicate a strong desire for a home atmosphere.
IMAGINATION: This block indicates how a player uses their imagination. Life is full of circles. If a player draws a face of an animal or person, they show a liking for pets or friends. If they draw an object, such as a bowling ball, they are inventive.

17

Game Variations Suggestions

1. At the end of the activity, the LEADER should provide this Disclaimer: The information presented concerning each DOODLE has little or no scientific basis.

2. Suggest other possibilities for DOODLES.

3. Allow in depth time for players to explain their DOODLES.

Group Game
Name Game
Equipment:
Paper and Pen or Pencil

fantasy go — around

5-14 Players
High School to Adult
Play Area:
Indoor or Outdoor

To Begin

All of the players form a circle. Players may sit on the floor, in chairs or at a desk. Players face toward the center and line up slightly more than arms length apart. The LEADER is crucial in this game. The LEADER will distribute a half sheet of paper and a pencil/pen to each player in the circle. The LEADER is encouraged to participate.

See Appendix C, Page 141 for sample sheets.

Next

Each player will write down a "FANTASY" on the piece of paper. Players will require adequate time to think about their FANTASY. The FANTASY should be something that they have wanted to do or have dreamed of doing. The FANTASY can be anything, real or fanciful, so long as it is something that the person has a desire to do. Once completed, the FANTASY will be read to the other players (use good taste). A couple of sentences are recommended. This works best if other players do not know about the

Setup

X = Players
O = Leader

Third

FANTASY.
The LEADER collects all of the sheets of paper and then shuffles them up so that there is no particular order to how they are arranged. The LEADER should read through each "FANTASY" quickly to become familiar with the content. The LEADER then reads each FANTASY out loud to the group. It is permissible for group members to point at one another attempting to guess which FANTASY belongs to each player. Individual players must not, however, reveal their own

Rules

FANTASY at this time.
Once all of the FANTASIES have been read, the LEADER slowly reads each FANTASY one more time. This time, as each FANTASY is read, the group attempts to match the player to the FANTASY. After all guesses are made, the player whose FANTASY was read owns up to their FANTASY. That player may want to share additional information. The game continues until all FANTASIES are read and each player has "owned" their own FANTASY.

18

Game Variations Suggestions

1. This game requires a strong LEADER who is familiar with team building techniques and processing.
2. Instead of a FANTASY, Players may write down a TRUTH or a LIE, something interesting or strange that no one else knows about them, a dream, a childhood experience, etc.

Guessing Game
Name Game

Equipment:
Pen and Paper

4-15 Players
High School to Adult

Play Area:
Desks or Flat Area

two truths and a lie

To Begin

Players sit in a circle (chairs or on the ground). The LEADER joins the circle and gives each player a piece of paper and a pen or pencil. Each player is instructed to prepare three statements about themselves. The LEADER also participates. Two of the statements must be TRUTHS. One statement will be a LIE.

Next

Once the statements have been completed, players (one at a time) will share their three statements in any order with the group. The object of the game is to for the players to figure out which statement is the LIE. The guessing players can ask questions and can confer with each other. The LEADER should ask for a consensus by a voice or hand count. The player will then reveal the LIE and perhaps share more information about the TRUTHS.

Setup

X X X
X   X
X   L
X   X
X   X
X X X

X= Players
L= Leader

Third

It is important for the LEADER to provide ample time for the players to prepare their statements. It is much easier for players to think of TRUTHS. Statements should be two sentences or more and contain some detail.
Good Example: I once spent a night camping on a sandbar with 40 clowns. We were on a river canoe trip.
Bad Example: I like Coke more than Pepsi.
Sometimes the best LIE is to think of something a family member or friend may have done.

Rules

Players should not share a statement that other players already know to be true or false.

Players must answer questions about their statements when asked.

Once a player reveals their TRUTHS and the LIE, players and the LEADER are encouraged to ask more questions to learn about the player.

Players can share their statements in any order.

Game Variations Suggestions

1. Players must take the time to write down their statements for this game to be more powerful. It is too easy to forget one of the statements.

2. A variation is to play a version called TWO TRUTHS AND A DREAM WISH. the DREAM WISH is something they wish to do.

Team Building
Problem Solving
Equipment:
None

king frog

5-14 Players
Middle School to Adult
Play Area:
Indoor or Outdoor

To Begin

The LEADER of the game has the players arrange themselves close together in a circle while sitting. One player is chosen to be the KING FROG from within the circle. The LEADER explains and demonstrates the group ACTION for this game. Once demonstrated, the KING FROG and all of the players in the circle repeat the ACTION. The ACTION consists of six steps: slapping the knees twice with palms down, clapping the hands twice and snapping the thumb and middle finger of the right hand and then snapping the thumb and middle finger of the left hand.

Next

Once the players have learned the ACTION, the LEADER explains and demonstrates each of the other VERBAL ACTIONS that will be said loudly by players in the game. These VERBAL ACTIONS will be practiced one at a time until the sequence of all of the VERBAL ACTIONS has been learned. VERBAL ACTION sequence: "ONE FROG", "TWO EYES", "FOUR LEGS", "IN A PUDDLE", "KER PLUNK", "KER PLUNK".

Setup

X
X   X

X   XX L

X   X
X

X = Players
O = Leader
XX = King Frog

Third

When the players get to the finger snapping part of the ACTION, the KING FROG says loudly, "ONE FROG". All players repeat the ACTION with the next player to the left of the KING FROG saying "TWO EYES" at the snap of the fingers. ACTION continues with the next player to the left saying, "FOUR LEGS". ACTION continues with the next player to the left saying, "IN A PUDDLE". The next player will say, "KER PLUNK". This is followed by another, "KER PLUNK". When a VERBAL ACTION sequence is completed with no mistakes, it is considered ONE FROG. The game continues.

Scoring

The goal is to see how many FROGS the group can complete. When a mistake occurs, the KING FROG starts the game over from the beginning.
2 FROGS: 4 EYES, 8 LEGS, 2 - IN A PUDDLE, and 4 - KER PLUNKS
3 FROGS: 6 EYES, 12 LEGS, 3 - IN A PUDDLE, and 6 - KER PLUNKS
4 FROGS: 8 EYES, 16 LEGS, 4 - IN A PUDDLES, and 8 - KER PLUNKS
5 FROGS: 10 EYES, 20 LEGS, 5 - IN A PUDDLE, and 10 - KER PLUNKS

20

Game Variations Suggestions

1. Large groups can play. Space each group of 7-12 players around a room. Give them time to practice the ACTIONS and the KING FROG sequence. After 5 to 10 minutes, select one team to demonstrate their team work while the other team/s circle around them. Provide each team with one or more KING FROG opportunities.

colander game

To Begin

The LEADER of the game has the players arrange themselves close together in a circle. Players sit (floor or chairs). The LEADER asks each player, one player at a time (in a clockwise direction) to carefully pick a vegetable and clearly name the vegetable out loud. No two players can select the same vegetable. The LEADER will also pick a vegetable. Each player should repeat their vegetable name a couple of times.

Next

The LEADER asks each player (in a clockwise direction) to carefully pick an action to symbolize their vegetable. Example: Potato... thumbs and forefingers together. No two players can select the same action. (The action does not have to make sense). When done, each player should repeat the name of their vegetable and demonstrates the action. Players should remember as many vegetables and actions as possible from the other players.

Setup

X X X
X   X
X   X
                     L
X= Players
X   L= Leader   X
X   X
X   X   X

Third

Players must always start with their "vegetable and action" and continue with someone else's "vegetable and action". The LEADER wears the colander. During the game, no one can show teeth! Each player must speak with their teeth covered by their lips. The colander will be worn by players who show teeth or by players who make a mistake with the "vegetable and action" sequence. The LEADER begins with his/her "vegetable and action" and follows quickly with someone else's "vegetable and action".

To Play

The player whose "vegetable and action" was identified, responds with his/her "vegetable and action" and follows quickly with someone else's "vegetable and action". This sequence continues unless a mistake is made and the colander has passed to the new leader who wears it while starting the game over. The action should be quick.

21

Game Variations Suggestions

1. Play using fruit, animals, or other items.
2. Prepare in advance names of vegetables (or other items) on sheets of paper for each player.

3. Concern: Leaders should watch out for a player who is struggling (and not having fun) as opposed to a player who is struggling and laughing so hard that his/her teeth are always showing.

Competitive Game
Team Building
Equipment:
Cups and Tag Board

bug racing

4-64 Players
Upper Elem. to Adult
Play Area:
Indoor or Outdoor

To Begin

This is a "mini" single elimination tournament with two or three players in each bracket to start the game. (Subsequent brackets will have two players per bracket). The tournament brackets must be set up once the number of players is determined. (Single Elimination - See Tournament Chapter - page 133). The "racing" board must be set up with a one meter circle and a three meter circle drawn on the Tag Board. Each player is given a cup with a lid by the LEADER of the

Next

game.
Each player must take their cup outside to areas of the environment where they can locate and capture one "crawling" bug. Each player should look for the fastest crawling bug that they can find. Bugs may not fly or hop..... only crawl. Only one bug is permitted per cup (10 ants in a cup does not count). Players return to the tournament room with their bug. Players should be told to avoid showing or describing their bugs to each other until the game starts.

Setup

Bug Racing Board

3 Meter Circle

1 Meter Circle

Third

The LEADER will place each player's name (and maybe the bug's name) at random on the first round of brackets of the tournaments (exp. Mike - Lightning). The tournament brackets may be placed on another sheet of tag board, a black board or a white board. When all of the brackets have been filled, the tournament can begin. The LEADER will select a player to assist with keeping the brackets updated after each contest. The game starts with the LEADER calling out the names of the contestants for each contest.

To Play

Each player called to compete will place their cup (with bug) face down in the one meter circle of the tag board (racing board). The LEADER will tap each cup and then quickly pick the cups off the board. The first bug to crawl past the three meter circle is the winner and advances to the next round. Action continues until the fastest bug is recognized as the champion. When play is completed, players should return their bugs to the locations where they were initially found.

22

Game Variations Suggestions

1. Players should "re-capture" their own bugs after a contest to avoid their bug getting injured.
2. If a bug is injured after the first round, a player may borrow a "defeated" bug to compete.
3. It is the final decision of the LEADER if a bug is disqualified due to flying or hopping.
4. Strategies develop if the game is played again.

Team Building
Problem Solving
Equipment:
15"-18" pieces of rope per player

human knots

5-15 Players
Upper Elementary to Adult
Play Area:
Indoor or Outdoor

To Begin

All of the players stand in a circle, shoulder to shoulder. A LEADER will direct the action. Each player gets a 15-18 inch piece of rope. Once the game begins, each player will reach forward to the center of the circle with both hands. One hand will be holding onto the rope. Each player then will grab the rope of another player with their free (empty) hand.

Next

No two players should be holding unto the rope of each other. Also, no player should grab hold of the rope of the player next to them. Finally, all ropes should be held by only one other hand. It may be necessary for the LEADER to rearrange some of the hands (and ropes) before the game begins.

Setup
X = Players
L = Leader

X X X X
X   X
X   X
Setup   L
X   X
X   X
X X X

Third

Once all of the players have joined together, the KNOT of ropes (and hands) must be untangled. This is accomplished by players working together to untie the KNOT. Players may step under or over other players arms or legs.

Objective

Players continue to untangle the KNOT without releasing their grips on the ropes they are holding! Occasionally, the outcome will be two interconnecting circles. At a point, there may be a tangle which prevents the KNOT from being untied. KNOT-AID can be administered (a momentary break in hands). KNOT-AID should allow the group to break and reconnect one set of hands at a time until success can be achieved and the next game started.

23

Game Variations Suggestions

1. Instead of players using ropes, they can hold hands.

2. If ropes are used instead of hands, more players can participate at one time. Maximum number is still 15. This works well with older participants.

Problem Solving
Team Building
Equipment:
Markers with Arrows

traffic jam

8-10 Players
Middle School to Adult
Play Area:
Indoor or Outdoor

To Begin

This is a group challenge game. Eight to ten players are required. The players organize themselves into two groups of four (or five). The LEADER explains that the goal of the game is for the players on the left side of the intersection to end up in the places on the right side of the intersection and vice versa. At the conclusion of the game, the intersection will be empty.

Next

Both groups face the empty intersection. One group stands on the squares to the left of the "empty intersection". The other group stands on the squares to the right side of the "empty intersection." The LEADER asks each group if any one has played this game before. (Those players continue to play but must not talk or share information to assist the group in solving the TRAFFIC JAM).

Setup

Empty Intersection

Third

1. Only one player can move at a time.
2. Players cannot move backwards.
3. Players may move into an empty space in front of them.
4. A player may move around another player who is facing them into an empty space (including the "Intersection").
5. Players cannot move around another player facing the same direction as them.

Note: It may be necessary for the entire group to start over.

Rules

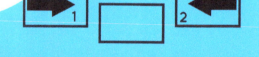

Example #1 (top): 1 or 2 may move into the empty space.

Example #2 (bottom): 1 may move into the empty space because two players are facing one another.

24

Game Variations Suggestions

1. Two or more groups can play this game simultaneously with additional Set-Up information.
2. Once the game starts, the LEADER should allow the players to decide how to solve the TRAFFIC JAM.

3. The LEADER should discuss the process and outcome of the game with all of the players.

Team Building
Guessing Game
Equipment:
1 Object & Sheet of Paper

what and where

8-20 Players
Middle School to Adult
Play Area:
Indoor or Outdoor

To Begin

Arrange the players into a small, tight circle with all of the players facing toward the center. Players can be sitting or kneeling. The LEADER must play as a member of the circle. The LEADER should be familiar with the game. Two items are needed to play the game. The first item is an OBJECT which can be almost anything. The second item is a sheet of paper (MAP). The OBJECT is the "WHAT" and the MAP is the "WHERE".

Next

When all of the players are sitting down, the LEADER picks up the OBJECT so everyone can see it and calls it by another name. For example, an apple can be called a pyramid! The LEADER then hands the OBJECT to the first player on their left and says, "THIS IS A PYRAMID!" The player receiving the OBJECT must respond, "A WHAT?" The LEADER repeats, "A PYRAMID!"

Setup

X= Players
L= Leader

Third

The first player then hands the OBJECT to the next player on the left and says, "THIS IS A PYRAMID!" The player receiving the OBJECT responds, "A WHAT?" The first player turns to face the LEADER and says, "A WHAT?" The LEADER replies, "A PYRAMID!" The first player turns back to the second player and says, "A PYRAMID!" This process continues as the OBJECT is passed around the cirlce until it is returned to the LEADER. The LEADER only practices with the first two players to help the players understand the game.

Objective

After practicing, the game begins. When the third player on the left has the OBJECT, the LEADER picks up the paper (MAP) and passes it to the first player on the right and says, "PYRAMIDS ARE FOUND IN EGYPT!" The player on the right responds, "WHERE?" The LEADER says, "EGYPT!" This process continues to the right around the circle until the MAP and the OBJECT return to the LEADER. Good Luck!

25

Game
Variations
Suggestions

1. Confusion usually develops at the junction of the circle when the WHAT and WHERE come together. This game should be processed at its conclusion.

2. The OBJECT and the MAP can be replaced by incorporating school mascots, holiday themes or strange and silly items.

barnyard

To Begin

All of the players form a circle. Players may sit on the floor, in chairs or at a desk. Players face toward the center and line up slightly more than arms length apart. The LEADER is crucial in this game. The LEADER will distribute a half sheet of paper and a pencil/pen to each player in the circle. The LEADER is encouraged to participate.

Next

The objective of this game is for all of the players to form teams of equal size. The LEADER begins by whispering the name of a barnyard animal to each player. It is important that the LEADER whispers the same amount of barnyard animals. The number of barnyard animals depends on the number of teams that the LEADER wants to create and the size of the group.

Setup

X = Players
O = Leader

Third

When all of the Players have been provided with the name of a barnyard animal (horse, goat, chicken, pig, cow, or duck, etc), the LEADER will explain to the group that when the game starts, all of the players will have to loudly make the sound of the barnyard animal that has been assigned to them. Along with the making the sound, all players may be asked to close their eyes and walk around the play area with their hands in front of them. They listen carefully and attempt to "group together" with all other players making the same sound.

Scoring

The LEADER will stop the game by yelling loudly when all players have "found" their teams. The LEADER will have each team demonstrate (loudly) their barnyard sound.

This can be a very fun game to randomly divide players into equal teams depending on the number of players involved and the number of teams desired. This is especially valuable when skill is not the primary pre-requisite for the activity to be successful.

Game Variations Suggestions

1. Hint for Getting Started: Fold a sheet of paper lengthwise in thirds. Write a "barnyard" animal on each third. Tape into a triangle.

2. Instead of barnyard animals, use familiar songs and have the players hum various songs i.e., Happy Birthday, Jingle Bells, Twinkle Little Star, I've Been Working on the Railroad, etc.

ah – so – ko

To Begin

The LEADER arranges the group into a tight circle with all players facing toward the center. The LEADER begins the game as the IT. The IT initiates the beginning action. There are three actions in the game. The first action is called the "AH" action. This action looks like a sharp salute with either the right or left hand touching the ITS forehead while the IT yells out "AH"! Which ever direction the AH hand is facing after the salute indicates who becomes the second IT. The new IT will either be on the immediate left or right of the first IT.

Next

The second IT must quickly follow up the AH action with the SO action. This action is done by quickly placing the right or left hand on their heart (the chest) with the palm facing down and loudly yelling out, "SO"! Which ever direction the SO hand is facing after the SO salute indicates who will become the third IT. The new IT will either be on the immediate left or right of the second IT. The player being pointed to at the completion of the SO salute becomes the third IT.

Setup

X = Players

X X X
X X
X X
X X
X X
X X
X X X

Third

The third IT must quickly follow up the SO action with the KO action. This action is done by quickly extending the right or left hand, palm verticle with the thumb up and performing a karate chop while yelling out "KO" and clearly pointing to another player around the circle. The player being pointed to at the completion of the KO karate chop becomes the next IT.

Continue Play

The AH-SO-KO actions with the accompanying sounds continue at a rapid pace. If a mistake is made or a player is slow to react, the player or players making the mistake will step back from the circle. The main circle continues to move closer together. After a mistake, the player who last made a correct action quickly starts the AH-SO-KO game again with the AH action. The game is completed when there are three or four players remaining.

27

1. After half of the players have been eliminated, a second circle can be formed and a second AH-SO-KO game can be started. Additional players may enter the second game as the first game continues until a player loses a second time.
2. Participants walk, shuffle or move in a clockwise rotation as the game progresses.

Competitive Game
Guessing Game
Equipment:
Coin & Long Table & Chairs

up jenkins

10-20 Players
Middle School to Adult
Play Area:
Indoor or Outdoor

To Begin

A LEADER arranges the players into two even numbered teams. Once teams are determined, each team will sit opposite of the other team at a long table. The LEADER stands at the front of the table. A device for scoring should be available for the LEADER (chalk board, tag board, large sheet of paper, etc.).

Next

Teams flip a coin to determine which team will go first. Each team "numbers off" from one to the total number of players on the team. The first player is GUESSER #1, the second player is GUESSER #2, and so on. All of the players from the coin flip winning team place their hands under the table. One player from that team takes the coin in one of his/her hands and also places both hands under the table.

Setup

X= Players L= Leader

X X X X X   X X   X X

L

X X X X X   X X   X X

Third

Players pass or pretend to pass the coin back and forth (under the table) among teammates. After fifteen to thirty seconds, the LEADER yells out, "UP JENKINS"! When "UP JENKINS" is yelled out, all of the players on the team must bring their elbows up on the table with fists clenched, palms up facing the other team. One player will be holding the coin.

Scoring

GUESSER #1 must decide which hand the coin is in. The GUESSER is encouraged to get information from teammates. The GUESSER attempts to expose the coin on the first guess. The GUESSER keeps guessing until successful. Each guess is added up for a GUESSER score. Action continues back and forth until all GUESSERS from both teams have had an opportunity to play. The LEADER keeps score. The team with the lowest score wins.

28

Game Variations Suggestions

1. Elimination method of scoring: The GUESSER attempts to uncover all of the empty hands before uncovering the coin. High score wins.

2. During the middle of the game, have the players on the ends of each team switch to the middle positions around the table so they will be more involved in the game.

Team Building
Problem Solving
Equipment:
None

scare bear

10-30 Players
High School to Adult
Play Area:
Indoor or Outdoor

To Begin

All of the players form a large, tight circle facing toward the center. The game requires two LEADERS who are familiar with the game. One player volunteers to be the GUESSER. The GUESSER leaves the play area with the second LEADER where they cannot hear the first LEADER. The first LEADER explains to all of the players in the circle how the game is to be played. The object of the game is for the GUESSER to guess which player is the SCARE BEAR. The GUESSER returns to the circle once the rules have been explained.

Next

The GUESSER has three chances to guess which player is the SCARE BEAR. The GUESSER stands on the edge of the circle and counts, "1, 2, 3". On "3", all of the players, who close their eyes during the count, jump into the circle and loudly growl and act like a bear. The GUESSER picks a SCARE BEAR. He/she will be wrong. A second time, "1, 2, 3". On "3", all of the players (with eyes closed) jump into the circle and loudly growl and act like a bear. The GUESSER will be wrong again. On attempt three, no matter who the GUESSER selects, they will be correct. The GUESSER gets congratulated.

Setup

X = Players L = Leader
G = Guesser

IT

Third

Players need to over react, to be loud and to pretend that they are the SCARE BEAR. It is also important that each player close their eyes when the GUESSER starts counting and open them when they jump into the circle. The player selected as the SCARE BEAR leaves the room. The first LEADER asks for a SCARE BEAR volunteer. After awhile someone suggests that the first GUESSER should be the SCARE BEAR because no one would guess him/her. The player agrees and the next GUESSER returns to the circle.

To End

Players close their eyes as the GUESSER counts, "1, 2, 3". On "3", all players jump into the circle growling and acting like a bear. The GUESSER picks a SCARE BEAR (NOT the former GUESSER). A second time, "1, 2, 3". On "3", the players jump into the circle growling and acting like a bear. The GUESSER picks a second SCARE BEAR (NOT the former GUESSER). On the third attempt, when the GUESSER says "3", all of the players just quietly stand in place. The "new" SCARE BEAR will jump into the middle screaming like a bear and realize that everyone else is quiet.

29

Game Variations Suggestions

1. The LEADERS should select a volunteer who is outgoing, loud and who can take a good joke.
2. More than one volunteer can be selected if time permits.
3. The LEADER needs to clearly explain the objective and rules of the game to the Players if this game will work.

Collective Score
Problem Solving
Equipment:
1 marker per player to stand on

birthday line-up

12-50 Players
Upper Elementary to Adult
Play Area:
Indoor or Outdoor

To Begin

All of the players form a large circle. Players face toward the center and line up slightly more than shoulder length apart. The LEADER takes a position on the circle among the other players. All of the players and the LEADER are given a marker. A marker can be a piece of carpet approximately 12" by 18". (A sheet of paper can be used).

Next

The LEADER explains to all of the players that the object of the game is for everyone to line-up in the order of the month and day of their birth (age of the player does not matter). However, none of the players are allowed to speak or make any mouth movements to tell other players their birthday. Each player places their marker on the floor and stands slightly behind it or on it. From this point until the end of the game, players can only stand on the markers and must move from marker to marker.

Setup
X = Players

Third

This is a game of strategy and balance. The LEADER remains on the same marker for the entire game but all of the other players may have to move. The LEADER starts by telling everyone his/her birthday (month and day) and becomes the starting point for the line-up. At a signal from the LEADER, all players attempt to line-up in sequence, clockwise or counter-clockwise around the circle using the LEADER'S birthday as the key for line-up movement.

Rules

Players may communicate with their hands, arms, fingers and head only. When all of the players think they are in the correct place, the LEADER repeats loudly his/her birthday and each player (in sequence) around the circle loudly announces their birthday. If a player is out of place, they must find the correct space in the line-up. This will require the other players to move to make the correction.

30

Game Variations Suggestions

1. There are many possible variations for this game. The LEADER may want to start the game by having everyone line up by age. The LEADER may also want players to line up alphabetically by month of birth or by day of birth. Players can line up by the State (or country) they were born in, or the City that they grew up in.

Team Building
Collective Score
Equipment:
None

singin in the sun

12-50 Players
Upper Elementary to Adult
Play Area:
Indoor or Outdoor

To Begin

Players are arranged in a circle or an "egg" shaped circle with the LEADER clearly visible to all of the players. The LEADER must be familiar with the song, "Singin' in the Sun" (See Appendix H- Page 145) . This game includes words and action. The LEADER must sing the chorus of "Singing in the Rain" to the participants. The LEADER may have to demonstrate the song chorus twice (or more). All of the players will then sing the chorus with the LEADER one more time.

Next

The Song:
I'm singing in the sun
Just singing in the sun
What a glorious feelin'........

The LEADER will stop or pause after the word feelin'....

The LEADER should encourage players to "dance" to the song as well as sing.

Setup

X = Players
O = Leader

Third

This time, when the entire group hesitates or pauses at the word feelin'..... The LEADER will shout out. " Elbows up!" All of the players will raise their arms high with their elbows pointed forward. The LEADER and all of the players will begin the song again (elbows still up). When the entire group gets to the word "feelin'.....", there is a hesitation/pause and the LEADER will shout out "Knees bent!" All of the players will bend their knees and keep their elbows up.

Objective

The LEADER and the players will sing the entire chorus again. When the song gets to the word feelin'.... the LEADER will shout out the next command. "Stomach out!" The song continues with players and the LEADER demonstrating all of the commands. Two additional commands are given by the LEADER, "Bottom back!" and finally, "Tongue out!" The game ends when all of the players and the LEADER are singing and performing all of the commands at one time.

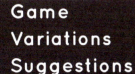

31

**Game
Variations
Suggestions**

1. There are many "contortions" and variations that the LEADER can select.

2. If possible, piano or guitar accompaniment adds support for those who do not like to sing.

3. A great game to start a game session or in a camp environment.

Competitive Game
Guessing Game
Equipment:
None

killer

12-30 Players
Middle School to Adult
Play Area:
Indoor or Outdoor

To Begin

All of the players scatter throughout the play area. It is better to have a smaller area than an area too large. Players stand in assorted directions with their eyes closed and their arms behind their backs with their fingers joined. The LEADER will walk around the play area and firmly squeeze one player's hands. This player becomes the KILLER. The Leader has all of the players open their eyes and announces that a KILLER has been chosen.

Next

At a "START" command from the LEADER, all of the players move at random through the group, shaking hands and introducing themselves to the other players. When the KILLER shakes hands with someone, he/she may silently "kill" that player by winking at them. Note: the KILLER does not have to wink every time they shake hands with another player.

Setup

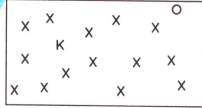

X = Players
O = Leader
K = Killer

Third

When a player is "winked at", they continue to walk through the crowd for three to five seconds. At that point, they fall to the ground, dying with great drama! The "killed" player remains in that position for the rest of the game. The game ends when either the KILLER "murders" all of the players, or if the KILLER"S identity is discovered.

Rules

If a player (who is not dead) suspects who the KILLER is, they raise their hand and loudly shout, "I know the KILLER"! If another player also knows the KILLER (or thinks they know), they raise their hand and also shout, "I know the KILLER"! Both players then count "1, 2, 3" and quickly point to the suspected KILLER. If they are correct, the game is over. If they point to two different people, they both must fall down and die on the spot, even if the KILLER has been pointed to by one player. The game continues.

32

Game
Variations
Suggestions

1. The players who are not the KILLER have to be careful not to wink.

2. The "wink" should be obvious.

3. Select two KILLERS if there are twenty or more players.

4. Encourage KILLERS to wink often and to not let the game "drag on".

Guessing Game
Competitive Game
Equipment:
Large Blanket or Parachute

who's there?

12-30 Players
High School to Adult
Play Area:
Indoor or Outdoor

To Begin

All players form a tight circle around the LEADER. Each player introduces themselves by providing the group with their first name and an activity that they enjoy. For example: "My name is Mike and I like to Mountain Bike" or "my name is Rachel and I like to Read" or "my name is Katie and I like to fly Kites". The activity that each player selects must start with the first letter of their first name. Duplication of activity interests may be possible but should be discouraged.

Next

Once everyone has introduced themselves, quickly go around the circle one more time. The LEADER then divides the players into two groups (be creative). A blanket or parachute is erected and secured lengthwise about four feet high. Each group moves to one side of the barrier and takes a kneeling or sitting position. No players should be able to see players from the other team over or around the sides of the barrier.

Setup

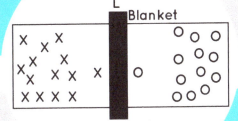

X = Team A
O = Team B
L = Leader

Third

The LEADER explains the rules. Each player from each team will get two opportunities to determine "WHO'S THERE?". The LEADER will keep score during the game. To start, each team selects one player to take a turn. The players selected from each team kneel close to the blanket facing the other team (which they cannot see). The LEADER will then say, "One, Two, Three, UP!" Each player "pops up", looks directly at the opposing player and quickly yells out the first name of that player. The first player to identify the other player wins a point for their team.

Scoring

Each player only gets one guess. If both players are wrong or don't know each other's names, they introduce themselves (and activity) once more. Two more players are selected and the game continues until every player has had two opportunities to guess, "WHO'S THERE?" Each team is encouraged to remember and share names with team members for the second round. Teams should also mix up the sequence of players selected to guess but to make sure that each player gets the same opportunity to guess, "WHO'S THERE?".

33

Game Variations Suggestions

1. A third round can be played with each player guessing the opposing players activity.
2. The losing player joins the winning team. The team with the most players after two rounds wins.
3. Players can guess other information about opposing players: home towns, favorite TV shows or movies, songs, pet names, etc.

Equipment:
None

howdy, neighbors!

Play Area:
Indoor or Outdoor

To Begin

There must be an even number of players to play this game. All of the players arrange themselves around a circle and next to a partner facing outward, away from the center of the circle. Couples (partners) should link inside arms. One couple is chosen to be the IT couple. The IT couple stands outside the circle.

Next

The IT couple, with elbows linked, walks around the circle. The IT couple walks until they come to a couple they wish to challenge. The IT couple stops, faces the couple they are challenging, bow together and say, "HOWDY, NEIGHBORS!" The challenged couple bows and repeats the greeting, "HOWDY, NEIGHBORS!" The greeting is repeated by both sets of partners three times. After the third greeting, both the IT and the challenged couples begin walking in opposite directions around the circle with elbows still linked.

Setup

XX XX XX
XX   XX
XX   XX
XX   XX

# Setup
XX= IT

XX   XX
XX   XX
XX   XX
XX XX XX XX

Third

When the two partner "teams" meet, the couples stop and face each other. The outside partners hold hands with the other partner team while keeping the inside arms linked. The IT couple in unison bends their knees and say, "HOW DO YOU DO? The non-IT couple then bends their knees and replies, "HOW DO YOU DO?" This is repeated three times. Each couple then drops hands with the other couple. The non IT couple raises their hands to form an arch while the IT couple walks under their raised arms.

To End

Each couple continues around the circle with arms linked. The first couple to return to the open spot left by the challenged couple will kneel down in the vacant space. The last couple to the open spot becomes the new IT couple and starts the next round by challenging any couple still standing. A couple that is kneeling cannot be challenged. The game ends when all the couples have been challenged. If the IT couple is having difficulty relinquishing the IT position, they can pick a kneeling couple to take their place.

**Game
Variations
Suggestions**

1. With large groups over 30, partner teams can arrange themselves in a circle with alternating couples facing inward and outward. A game can be played inside the circle as well as outside the circle at the same time.

Team Building
Collective Score

Equipment: Speakers & Music
4 Cones for Boundaries

dancing dracula

15-40 Players
Upper Elementary to Adult
Play Area:
Indoor or Outdoor

To Begin

Select music that players enjoy or music based on a theme. The music should be loud and lively. This is important so that the players do not hear the movement of the DRACULAS. The players scatter throughout the play area standing away from other players. When the music begins, players dance in place. The LEADER may participate as a player.

Next

Two players are chosen to be the first DRACULAS. Another person is picked to be in charge of turning the music on and off during the game. Once the music is turned on, it should stay on for 30 to 60 seconds. When it is abruptly turned off, it should remain off just long enough for the DRACULAS to do their "Dracula" work.

Setup

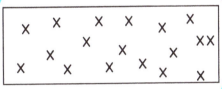

X = Players
XX = IT

Third

When the music starts to play, all of the players start to dance while keeping their eyes closed. The DRACULAS walk around with eyes open, looking for a victim. When the music stops, the dancers (players) also stop, holding their dancing pose. The DRACULAS, in unison, clap their hands twice near the victim's head and scream. The DRACULAS must be careful not to scream directly into their victims ears or to touch or grab the "victim".

To End

DRACULAS may gang up on victims. Once a victim has been identified and "scared" by the DRACULAS, they become a DRACULA too. The music starts again, the players dance and the action continues. The game ends when there are no more victims left and then a new game begins!

35

Game Variations Suggestions

1. The LEADER may want to teach dance steps or a particular dance prior to the game starting.

2. Blindfolds can be used but be careful. The use of blindfolds involves trust.

hustle bustle

To Begin

The LEADER will select this game for groups who are still trying to learn each others names. The players form a circle, standing slightly more than shoulder width apart. The LEADER will be a part of the circle and should be familiar with the game. One player with an accurate watch will be asked to be the TIMER. The TIMER stands behind the LEADER. The player on each side of the LEADER is a TEAM CAPTAIN.

Next

The LEADER explains to the players that HUSTLE BUSTLE is a "speed game" that involves remembering first names. The LEADER begins by stating his/her first name so everyone can hear it. The player to the left of the LEADER immediately tells the group his/her first name. This continues all around the circle. If a player in the circle cannot hear a name clearly, that person can quickly yell out, "Repeat!"

Setup

```
      X   X   X
   X           X
 X               X
X                 O
X                L T
X                 O
 X               X
   X           X
      X   X   X
```

T= Timer
L= Leader
O= Captains

Third

After all players have stated their names, the LEADER informs the group that all names will be repeated one more time (and one name at a time) with the TIMER keeping track of how fast the group can complete the task. Once completed, the LEADER announces the group time. The LEADER then asks the group if they can record a faster time. The LEADER should allow the group to come to an agreement if changes are to be made. Two attempts should be given by the TEAM CAPTAIN to the left and then two attempts should be given by the TEAM CAPTAIN to the right.

Extra

Players remain in the same circle. One last challenge: When the LEADER says "start", each TEAM CAPTAIN starts again by saying the players name next to him/her with a race around the circle back to the LEADER. It is important that players clearly pronounce their names. For more challenge, players can pronounce their first and last names, their nicknames or their hometowns.

36

Game Variations Suggestions

1. This game should stimulate discussion. The LEADER should listen, react to suggestions but be careful to not take over the action. 2. Once the game is completed

encourage a volunteer (or two) to go-around the circle and name as many names as possible.
3. Discuss competing: was there competition?

Name Game
Problem Solving
Equipment:
None

name by name

15-40 Players
Upper Elementary to Adult
Play Area:
Indoor or Outdoor

To Begin

The LEADER will select this game for players who are still trying to learn each other's names. The players form a circle, standing slightly more than shoulder width apart. The LEADER will be a part of the circle and should be familiar with the game. The LEADER begins by stating his/her first name so everyone can hear it.

Next

The player to the left of the LEADER immediately tells the group his/her first name. This continues all around the circle. If a player in the circle cannot hear a name clearly, that person can quickly yell out, "Repeat!" After all of the names have been said, the LEADER explains the challenge.

Setup

X = Players
O = Leader

Third

At a signal from the LEADER, all players must quickly rearrange themselves so that the circle becomes alphabetical by first name. There is no talking, no signing or gesturing (visually indicating letters), no showing cell phone information, ID cards, etc. Players may assist other players by pointing to a spot but the challenge is for individuals to place themselves in the circle in the correct alphabetical order. They must remember names!

Playing

Once the group has moved and reformed, the LEADER announces that Round One is completed. Starting with the LEADER, all players again say their first name. If players are out of sequence, they stay where they are and corrections need to be made in Round Two. A Round Three and Round Four may be necessary.

37

Game Variations Suggestions

1. This game is not recommended if players are already familar with the names of other players.
2. For workshops or for more advanced players, substitute home towns, school nicknames, etc.
3. Once the game is completed, encourage a volunteer (or two) to go-around the circle and name as many names as possible.

Problem Solving
Guessing Game
Equipment:
4 Cones for Boundaries

prui

15-30 Players
High School to Adult
Play Area:
Indoor or Outdoor

To Begin

All of the players scatter throughout the play area. Players stand with their eyes closed and their arms behind their backs. The LEADER will walk around the play area and firmly squeeze one of the player's hands. This player becomes the PRUI. When the game starts, the PRUI will walk around the play area with their eyes open but must not speak at any time. The LEADER does not play the game but is responsible for keeping the players in bounds during the game.

Next

At a given signal from the LEADER, all of the players try to find the PRUI. Players walk around the play area with their hands in front of them and their eyes closed (it's OK to peek a little if players feel nervous). Players attempt to BUMP into other players while searching for the PRUI. The PRUI must allow other players to BUMP into him/her. With a large number of players, the PRUI must make an effort to let players find him/her. It makes the game more fun.

Setup

```
30 to   X  X  X    X     X    X
60          X  X        X       O
Feet      X  X  X
        X  L      X      X     X
```

30 to 60 Feet

X = Players
L = Leader
O = Prui

Third

When a player BUMPS into another player, they shake hands and one player says loudly, "PRUI?" If the other player responds "PRUI", the PRUI has not been found. Each player continues to look for the PRUI. If, however, a player calls out, "PRUI?" and receives no answer, they call out "PRUI" again. If there is no answer a second time, the PRUI has been found.

To End

When a player finds the PRUI, they join hands with the PRUI and open their eyes. The PRUI continues to grow larger. If a player BUMPS into a line of players with their hands joined (part of the PRUI), they must feel their way, (with their eyes closed) up arms, overheads and back down arms all the way to the end of the PRUI. At this point they will open their eyes, join the line and become part of the PRUI. When the last player joins the PRUI, the game is over.

38

Game

Variations

Suggestions

1. Be careful leading this game. Touching and playing with one's eyes closed require trust and careful demonstration.

2. The game can be played with two PRUIs.
3. The size of the play area should be small enough so that players can "bump" into each other quickly.

bumpity bump bump bump

To Begin

All the players form a large circle. Players face toward the center and line up shoulder length apart. One player is selected to be the IT. The game LEADER should be the first IT. The IT stands in the middle of the circle and tells everyone his/her name. All of the players in the circle then say in unison, "HI, (IT's name)". The IT responds by saying, "HI!" All new ITS must introduce themselves to the group this way.

Next

The IT tells everyone to introduce themselves to the players on their right and left sides. Players must remember the names. Once the names are known, the IT spins in a circle and clearly points to a player in the circle. At the same time that the IT points, the IT clearly calls out: "Left" or "Right" and quickly yells out: "BUMPITY, BUMP, BUMP, BUMP".

Setup

X = Players
O = Leader

Third

The Player pointed to has three seconds (or by the time the IT says "BUMPITY, BUMP, BUMP, BUMP" to yell out the correct name of the player to the right or left. If a player doesn't say the name correctly or the name quickly enough, he or she trades places with the IT in the center. The new IT is introduced. The first IT (the Leader) becomes a player by taking a position in the circle. The players re-introduce themselves and remember the names.

Playing

The game should move along quickly. As an added twist, the IT can spin and at any time randomly yell out "BUMPITY, BUMP, BUMP, BUMP" and everyone has to find a new spot in the circle. The IT who calls out "BUMPITY, BUMP, BUMP, BUMP" remains in the middle.

39

Game Variations Suggestions

1. The LEADER should spend time looking in the appendix for interesting KEY and MIME WORDS that fit the age level participating in the game.
2. It is important for the LEADER to emphasize that the players clearly mime their responses.
3. After a correct guess, the players can explain what they were acting out (this is fun).

Name Game
Team Building
Equipment:
None

growth circles

16-34 Players
High School to Adult
Play Area:
Indoor or Outdoor

To Begin

Players arrange themselves in a circle with enough distance for private space. The LEADER will be part of the circle if there is an odd number of players. Each player selects a partner (the player standing next to them). One of the partners steps in front of the other and faces the partner. Players should introduce themselves.

Next

The LEADER should come prepared with "story starters" or "sentences that need to be completed". A list has been prepared for the LEADER to view (See Appendix D - Page 142). The type of questions presented by the LEADER will depend on the type of group, age levels of the players and the purpose of the activity.

Setup

```
      X    X
   X  O  O  O   X
 X O            O X
X O             L
                   O X
 X O    X= Outside Circle
        O= Inside Circle
 X O    L= Leader      O  X
      O            O X
   X  O   O   O X
      X   X   X
```

X = Outside Circle
O = Inside Circle
L = Leader

Third

The LEADER starts by posing a question or statement to the entire group. Players on the outside of the circle have 30 seconds to answer. Their partners must listen and can ask questions to gain more information. At the end of the time limit, the inner circle of players answers the same question. It is important for the LEADER to keep on a consistent time schedule.

Playing

When time has expired, the inner circle rotates one (or two) spaces to the right. Players introduce themselves to their new partners. The LEADER poses a second question. The inner circle answers first. This pattern continues. This activity can go on for as long as desired, giving players the chance to have one on one discussions with many different people in the group.

40

Game

Variations

Suggestions

1. The LEADER needs to carefully consider the type and content of the questions asked.
2. At the end of the activity, players can volunteer to share information

about themselves that they learned from the GROWTH CIRCLE game.
3. The LEADER can allow in depth time for players to process this exercise.

Team Building
Problem Solving
Equipment:
Large Parachute, 20-40 Soft Objects

popcorn

20-30 Players
Lower Elementary to Adult
Play Area:
Indoor or Outdoor

To Begin

All of the players form a large circle around a "Game" parachute. Players face toward the center. A LEADER takes a position on the circle among the other players. All of the players grab hold of the parachute. If there are no handles, players may roll the edges of the parachute a couple of times for better grip. Two or three players volunteer to be CHASERS.

NOTE: A very large, durable blanket can be substituted for the parachute.

Next

All of the players and the LEADER lower the parachute to the ground. The LEADER explains to the players how POPCORN is prepared. One player is chosen to pour the "make believe" oil into the pan (the parachute). Another player is chosen to turn on the oven with a "Click". The LEADER then carefully places all of the balls or soft objects onto the pan.

Setup

C
X X X X
X
X
X X
C X O
X C
X X
X
X X X

X= Players
O= Leader
C= Chaser

Third

As the oil heats up, the LEADER and the players slowly and carefully begin to shake the parachute up and down. Simultaneously, each player moves from a kneeling to a standing position. As the oil "heats up", the shaking motion becomes more vigorous and the POPCORN begins to bounce up and down. The CHASERS get prepared to retrieve POPCORN that has popped out of the pan.

Continue Play

The players shake the parachute until all of the objects are bouncing in all directions. Most of the POPCORN will pop off the pan. The CHASERS return the balls to the parachute as quickly as possible. Once all of the corn and been popped and there are NO OLD MAIDS in the pan, the game is over and can be played again.

41

Game Variations Suggestions

1. The LEADER should spend time looking in the appendix for interesting KEY and MIME WORDS that fit the age level participating in the game.
2. It is important for the LEADER to emphasize that the players clearly mime their responses.
3. After a correct guess, the players can explain what they were acting out (this is fun).

elephant palm tree monkey

Equipment:
None

Play Area:
Indoor or Outdoor

To Begin

All of the players form a large circle. Players face toward the center and line up slightly more than shoulder length apart. The LEADER should begin as the first IT. The IT stands in the middle of the circle and leads a demonstration for each of the three poses: ELEPHANT, PALM TREE and MONKEY. Each pose involves three players. Every player in the circle should learn the poses before the game begins.

Next

The IT spins in a circle and clearly points at any player and calls out either, "ELEPHANT", "PALM TREE" or "MONKEY". The player pointed to and the players on each side must make the correct pose before the rest of the group can yell out "ELEPHANT, PALM TREE, MONKEY!" If the three players complete the pose in time, the IT spins around again and points at another player and gives them a pose command. If a mistake is made, the player who makes the mistake or the player who makes the biggest mistake is the new IT.

Setup
X = Players
O = IT

Actions

ELEPHANT: The player pointed to makes a trunk by bending forward at the waist, holding arms together and reaching toward the ground. The players on each side make huge ears with their arms and place them near the trunk of the ELEPHANT.
PALM TREE: The player pointed to becomes the tree trunk by extending both hands up high. The players on each side become the palm leaves by placing their hips near the trunk, extending their arms and bending away from the trunk.

Actions

MONKEY: The player to the left of the player pointed to becomes "HEAR NO EVIL" by covering their ears. The player pointed to becomes "SEE NO EVIL" and covers their eyes. The Player to the right of the player pointed to is "SPEAK NO EVIL" and covers their mouth.

(Hint: The sequence is in alphabetical order i.e., HEAR, SEE, SPEAK).

Game Variations Suggestions

1. Have the players that are selected to complete a pose make the sound of the animal or object.
2. Add more poses that require three participants: Race Car Driver

Quarterback and Wide receivers, Fire Hydrant with Dogs on each side, etc.
3. Play the game with two ITs

Team Building
Problem Solving
Equipment:
Large Blanket/Tarp/Parachute

Flippity Flip

20-30 Players
Middle School to Adult
Play Area:
Indoor or Outdoor

To Begin

The size of the large blanket, tarp or parachute is important. It should be large enough for all of the players to stand on at one time with one-third of the play space empty. All of the players form a line around the blanket. Players face toward the center. The LEADER takes a position on the line among the other players.

Next

All of the players must remain on the blanket while the entire group attempts to turn the blanket upside down so that everyone is standing on the opposite side.

Setup

X = Players L = Leader

X X X X X L X X X X X

BLANKET

Third

The LEADER must explain the rules prior to players stepping onto the blanket. Time can be provided for the players to discuss a strategy. The LEADER should monitor safety issues. Players should not sit up on shoulders of teammates. Once the game begins, the LEADER should not provide any information that helps the group solve the problem.

Rules

Once the game begins, all of the players must remain on the blanket at all times. This includes both hands and both feet.

If the LEADER observes a player step off the blanket, the challenge must start over from the beginning.

If a player (or players) have played the game before, the LEADER can ask them to participate but to not offer suggestions to help solve the game. They can also be blindfolded.

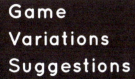

43

Game Variations Suggestions

1. Half of the group can be blindfolded. Blindfolded players should be provided a partner to assist them throughout the game. Only blindfolded players can touch the blanket.

2. Set a time limit.

3. Let the group play three or four times while the LEADER times each session.

Team Building
Problem Solving
Equipment:
None

lap sit

25-99 Players
Upper Elementary to Adult
Play Area:
Indoor or Outdoor

To Begin

This game requires a strong LEADER who is familiar with the game. All of the players gather together forming a tight circle while facing the center of the circle. The LEADER needs to be visible and loud (a large group may require the LEADER to have a megaphone).

Next

At the "START" command of the LEADER, players step forward until they are standing shoulder to shoulder. All players then turn and face to the right. It is very important that players stay in a circle that is as "round" as possible (not egg shaped). Players move sideways toward the center until they are standing heel-to-toe with the players in front of and behind them. Toes and heels should be touching.

Setup

X = Players
O = Leader

Third

It is advisable to have a demonstration with a very large group. Six or seven players can perform the demonstration in the center of the circle. It can also be helpful for each player to place their hands gently on the hips or the shoulders of the player in front of them. On a given signal from the LEADER, all players will sit back on the knees and thighs of the player behind them. Players need to sit back and not just bend their knees.

To End

All players must sit at the same time (Ready, one, two, three, SIT!). Once all of the players are sitting, the LEADER may have the players attempt to raise their hands and cheer, or even try something more challenging. On a signal from the LEADER, players take a step forward with their right foot, and then their left, etc. This is only successful if all players work together.

44

Game Variations Suggestions

1. With very large groups, it can be helpful if the LEADER has assistant leaders walking around the LAP SIT to assure that the circle is round and that players are lined up toe to heel.

2. Santa's Lap: All players are Santas and kids at the same time. When the lap sit is complete, all players sing one verse of "Jingle Bells".

medium

energy level

Quick Description

Tandem Juggling- unique step by step method for partners to learn to juggle together for 2-30 players and groups of two for middle school to adults. (3 objects per group)

Pyramids- group challenge for teams of five which involves duplicating various physical pyramids for 5-50 players for middle school to adults. (Pyramid diagrams)

Tree Ball- exciting small group challenge game played outside around a tree for 5-12 players for middle school to adults. (Tree and a special ball)

Bumper Ball- quick moving round robin competition for 6-10 players for elementary to adults. (3 tennis balls for every two players)

Noodle Face-Off- competitive face off with noodles and a balloon for 4-10 players for elementary to middle school. (Noodles for each player and balloons)

Group Juggling- game where players learn names, pass objects and work together as a team for 7-15 players for elementary to adults. (Soft objects to pass like balls or rings)

Onboard- small group problem solving challenge for 7-15 players for middle school to adults. (Platform)

Balloon Frenzy- spirited team competitive "frenzied" challenge for 8-40 players for elementary to adults. (Balloons)

Fence- challenging group undertaking involving trust for 8-20 players for middle school to adults. (Long bungee cord or taught rope)

Sherpa Walk- group team building and trust activity with minimum communication and is played with eyes closed for 6-80 players and teams of 8-15 for middle school to adults. (Maybe blindfolds)

New Musical Chairs- non elimination continuous action musical chair game for 10-20 players for all ages. (Chairs for each player minus one and music)

Raccoon Circles- series of games and challenges using webbing for 10-100 players and teams of 10-14 for elementary to adults. (Webbing for each group)

All Catch and Up Chuck- group "catching a ball" challenge for middle school to adults. (Ball for each player)

Tiny Teachings- activity where each player teaches another player something special that is later shared by the group for 10-20 players for high school to adult. (To be determined)

Fish Gobbler- game for children that involves tag, following commands and make believe for 12-40 players for young children. (Boundary markers)

Jack Be Nimble Relay- team relay that involves running, spinning and jumping for 20-60 players with teams of 6-10 per team for elementary to adults. (One noodle per team)

Needle and Thread Tag- quick one on one tag game in a group setting for 12-16 players for elementary to adults. (No equipment)

Laughing Logs- combination group challenge and relay game for 12-30 players for middle school to adults. (No equipment)

Popsicle Push-Ups- physical group problem to solve and accomplish for 12-40 players for middle school to adults. (No equipment)

Impulse- team guessing and competitive game which each player getting a chance to be a leader for 14-40 players for elementary to adults. (Cones and an object)

People to People- group name game with lots of quick movement for 20-50 players for middle school to adults. (Marker for each player)

Queen Bee Tag- group tag game with one "Key"

tagger and many helpers until everyone is tagged for 15-30 players for elementary to adults. (Boundary markers and balls)

SWAT- group game with a one on one sprint around the circle of players to avoid being swatted for 15-30 players for middle school to adults. (Rolled up newspaper and a frisbee)

Lemonade- problem solving and team guessing game that involves actors and guessers for 16-40 players for middle school to adults. (No equipment)

Skin the Snake- relay and trust game that involves laying down and getting back up as a team for 16-50 players for middle school to adults. (No equipment)

Snake Pit- one on one challenge between the snake and the mongoose in a circle of players for 16-30 players for middle school to adults. (Two rattles and a rolled up newspaper)

Alligator- fast moving group tag game for 20-30 players for all ages. (Parachute or large blanket)

Big Wind Blows- a group challenge game with leader commands for 20-30 players for all ages. (Parachute or large blanket)

Cat and Mouse- exciting "cat catch mouse" game for 20-30 players of all ages. (Parachute or large blanket)

Shark- group activity where the shark attempts to catch all of the players for 20-30 players for all ages. (Parachute or large blanket)

Touch and Go- series of sounds and commands that large groups must quickly respond to for 20-60 players for elementary to adults. (Noise maker and commands)

Four Square Relay- action packed team relay game that has all players in motion during play for 20- 60 players for all ages. (One chair per player and one balloon or ball)

Giants, Wizards, and Elves- group tag game where players change teams, mimic characters and attempt to get everyone on the same team for elementary to adults. (Boundary markers)

Do You Know Your Neighbor- group name game with lots of quick movement for 20-50 players for middle school to adults. (Marker for each player)

Quick Line-Up- fast moving competitive memory game for 20-40 players for middle school to adults. (No equipment)

Wave- amazing people to people cooperative effort to keep one player from sitting down for 20-40 players for middle school to adults. (One chair per player)

Who Started the Stampede- movement and guessing game where the it attempts to guess who starts the motion before being trampled for 20-60 players for middle school to adults. (No equipment)

Fire on the Mountain- movement game using music or chants that requires players to change partners for 21-51 players for middle school to adults. (Music)

Cookie Machine- a very large group relay game for 30-60 players for middle school to adults. (No equipment)

Problem Solving
Team Building

Equipment:
3 Objects Per Group

2-30 Players
Middle School to Adult

Play Area:
Indoor or Outdoor

tandem juggling

To Begin

Players select a partner. A LEADER selects one player (a partner) for a demonstration for all of the players to view. The LEADER and the PARTNER stand 10 - 15 feet apart while facing one another. One foot can be placed in front of the other (left foot if a player is right handed). Three similar objects are required to play the game. Tandem juggling is essentially using two hands - one from each player to juggle three objects.

Next

There are five actions for successful tandem juggling; 1) the toss, 2) the delayed toss, 3) the catch, 4) the delayed toss, and 5) the catch. The LEADER starts with one object in one hand which is carefully tossed underhand to the PARTNER who catches it in one hand. (Note: the throwing and catching hand is the same hand). The LEADER and the demonstrating PARTNER toss the object underhand back and forth a number of times to get comfortable with the toss and catch action.

Setup

X = Players

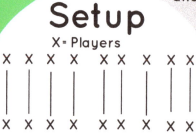

Third

The demonstration continues with a second object added. The second object is held in the tossing/catching hand of the PARTNER. The LEADER tosses the first object, which will be caught in one hand by the PARTNER. When the first object is in the air, the second object is tossed back to the LEADER and then the first object is caught. There is a clear delay before the second object is tossed. LEADER - toss first object

Playing

Practice this action a number of times before adding a third object. To complete the three-item juggle, the LEADER holds two objects in one hand while the PARTNER holds one object.
LEADER - toss first object
PARTNER - delayed toss of second object
PARTNER - catch first object
LEADER- delayed toss of third object
LEADER - catch second object
PARTNER- delayed toss of first object
PARTNER- catch third object...continue sequence

Game

Variations

Suggestions

1. After practicing, each group can demonstrate their skill to the other groups.
2. If players do not catch well, both hands can be joined together to form one hand.
3. When players have mastered the juggle, they can get fancy and toss through legs, behind backs or they can spin in a circle.

Problem Solving
Team Building
Equipment:
None

pyramids

5-30 Players
Middle School to Adult
Play Area:
Indoor or Outdoor

To Begin

Players form groups of five per group (if there is an odd number there can be six). The LEADER will present to each group a PYRAMID diagram (see Pyramid Diagrams - (See Appendix M - Page 149-160). These should be presented in sequential order. The LEADER can present them by 1) showing them to the groups from the Appendix diagrams or by scanning them and presenting them digitally.

Next

The groups scatter throughout the play area with sufficient room to accomplish each PYRAMID. Each PYRAMID will require all five players in a group to participate. Three players will actually complete the PYRAMID while the other two players serve as spotters. The LEADER may have to instruct groups on proper spotting techniques. Each PYRAMID requires all players to have a role in successfully completing the PYRAMID.

Setup

X = Players   O = Leader

Third

Each group will be presented with the same PYRAMID diagram. The objective is to complete the PYRAMID and have it look like the diagram. The LEADER will provide each group with 3 - 5 minutes to practice each PYRAMID. After the practice session, the LEADER will stop play and at a start signal have each group perform the PYRAMID one more time. A second objective is to have all of the groups remain in the PYRAMID position for five seconds at the same time.

Rules

Spotters must be present and active.
All players should have the opportunity to be part of the PYRAMIDS and to be spotters.
Players should participate without shoes.
It's OK to not successfully complete a PYRAMID.
At the conclusion of each PYRAMID, the LEADER can process what has just happened by asking players what they though/learned and can also point out observations about the process

49

Game Variations Suggestions

1. Safety is an issue. The LEADER must monitor each group to decide how many of the PYRAMIDS the groups are safely capable of completing.

2. Age and ability level of the players must be carefully considered.
3. Digital photos of group PYRAMIDS may be useful for future reference and processing.

Equipment:
Softball/Football/Soccerball

Play Area:
Big Tree or Flat Area

To Begin

Select a tall tree with many branches and a large play area around the trunk. Oaks, maples and some pines work best. There should not be any branches on the bottom 10 to 15 feet of the tree. The area under the tree should be flat and free from obstructions. You may want to remove any loose or dead branches. A ladder may be useful if the ball gets stuck in the tree. Fourteen-inch softballs, soccer balls or a football are recommended.

Next

Players form a large circle around the tree and face toward the center (tree trunk). One or two players should be positioned near the trunk. One player is chosen to start throwing the ball. That player should stand back from the tree and throw the ball high into the tree so the ball with ricochet and bounce off the branches as it comes down. Throwers can rotate throughout the game. It is important, however, that each thrower stand back from the tree to make the throw high and into the top of the tree.

Setup

X = Players   T = Thrower

Tree

Third

Once the ball is thrown into the tree, all of the players keep a close watch on it and try to catch the ball before it hits the ground. It is important for players to communicate with other players. If the ball is headed directly for someone, it is advisable for other players to gather around to assist in catching the ball in case it ricochets at the last moment.

To Play

One point is awarded to the group for each catch. The object is to see how many catches can be made in a row by the players (collective score). When the ball hits the ground, the score returns to zero. A "legal" catch must pass though the tree, making contact with at least one branch. After every three to five misses, the players should rotate, clockwise, one position to the left and around the trunk.

50

Game

Variations

Suggestions

1. Before the game starts, set a goal of ten or more catches in a row.
2. The smaller the ball, the more difficult the task.
3. Standing under the tree and toss-ing it up to touch a lower branch should be discouraged.

Problem Solving
Competitive Game
Equipment:
3 Tennis Balls per 2 Players

6-10 Players
Upper Elementary to Adult
Play Area:
Indoor or Outdoor

bumper ball

To Begin

This is a round robin tournament with each player playing all of the other players. Each game during each round is played at the same time on a flat play surface that has been set up in advance. In the example above, there are ten players with two players at each game on court (#A, #B, #C, #D and #E). Individual games take place while all of the players compete at the same time. If there is an odd number of players, there will be a bye each round. See (Round Robin - Tournament Chapter - page 133) for set up information.

Next

The LEADER determines the length between players based on age and ability. The LEADER prepares and posts all of the games for each round where players can view them. The LEADER also sets up a scoring system to keep track of wins, loses and ties. Each player sits with legs open or kneels behind the established starting lines. They each receive one tennis ball, which is placed on the ground in front of them. Because there are simultaneous games going on, there must be adequate distance between individual games.

Setup

X= Players   O= Leader
X | with Ball   X #A
X   X #B
X   X #C
X   X #D
X   20 to 30 Feet   X #E
              O

Third

One of the players from each team receives a third ball, which is held. At the start command, the third ball is rolled (not thrown or bounced) toward the stationary ball of the opposite player. If it hits the ball, the "roller" receives one point. If it misses, the ball is rolled back in an attempt to hit the first players stationary ball. Players keep track of how many hits they get. Each game lasts for one minute. When five seconds remain, the LEADER loudly counts down, "five, four, three, two, one, stop!"

Winning

The LEADER then asks players if they won, lost or tied. These results are recorded on a scoreboard. The second round starts as soon as players rotate to the next position with a different competitor. The LEADER shouts, "start" and the process is continued. Play lasts until every player has rotated and has played every other player.

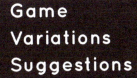

Game Variations Suggestions

1. Scoring: The LEADER quickly adds up the scores. Players get three points for each win, one point for a tie and zero points for a loss. In case of a tie, a tie breaker method can be used to determine the winner.

2. There should be extra balls available in case a ball gets by the players.

Team Building
Competitive Game
Equipment:
3 Inflated Ballons & (10) 4' Noodles

noodle face-off

6-14 Players
Middle School to Adult
Play Area:
Indoor or Outdoor

To Begin

Players are divided into two equal teams. A good method to accomplish this is to have all of the players find a partner about the same size as themselves. Line up the partners across from each other so they are facing their partners. Players in the lines should start by being shoulder to shoulder or close together. Intersperse larger and smaller partners throughout each line.

Next

A highly visible center line must be present. Both teams move close enough to each other but remain on their side of the center line. Once the game begins, the players may move around on their side of the line in either direction as the action dictates. Each player on each team is given a four foot section of a Noodle (it's a game device).

Setup
X = Players

Third

The Leader begins the action by tossing a fully inflated balloon high into the air near the center of both teams (near the center line). The Leader quickly moves to a spot on one end of the line to serve as the "referee" and to keep score. The goal of the game is for each team to FACE OFF and to use the Noodles to keep the balloon from: 1) touching any team members and 2) from landing on the ground on their side of the center line. This is done by the use of the Noodle and team work.

Rules

Players may not touch the balloon except with the Noodle and must remain on their side of the centerline. The balloon may only be moved or propelled by players striking the balloon when it comes close to them. More than one player may strike the balloon at one time.

A game is over when it touches a player or hits the ground. The first team to win two (or three) games is the winning team.

52

Game
Variations
Suggestions

1. A "mini" tournament can be established if there are four or eight teams. Use the Mueller Anderson format - (See Tournament Chapter - page 158).

2. Safety: The Leader must monitor for improper use of the Noodle. Players may not swing at or poke other players.

Equipment: Ropes/Tape for Boundry
Markers & Numbered Circles

Play Area:
Indoor or Outdoor

To Begin

The LEADER must prepare 30 circular objects by clearly numbering them from one to thirty. Paper plates or cut out paper circles can be used. The boundaries and the numbered objects must be prepared and placed as indicated in the organizational pattern above. Number 30 should end up farthest from the Start Line. (See Appendix J - Page 147) for a larger diagram of the set-up.

Next

Players meet with the LEADER away and out of site (if possible) from the organizational grid. The goal and challenge for the group is to approach the NUMBER TO NUMBER grid, touch all thirty numbered objects in sequential order (1 to 30) and to return past the Start Line as quickly and efficiently as possible. Once the players are informed of the goal, the group is given 2 - 3 minutes to work out a strategy. All planning must take place behind the start line.

Setup

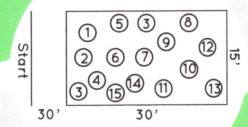

Rules

The entire group of players must begin and end behind the starting line.
Time begins when the first player crosses the line and ends when the last player returns. Only one player may enter the grid at a time. This includes arms reaching over the grid lines.
Penalty: 10 seconds added to the total time per offense.
Numbered Objects must be touched in sequence.
Penalty: 10 seconds added to the total time.
Numbered Objects may only be touched once.
Penalty: 10 seconds added to the total time.

Strategy

The players will have three to five attempts to reach their best time. All players must enter the playing area and leave the playing area for each attempt. This is a "team" challenge. The players will have two minutes to discuss and plan each attempt. The LEADER should refrain from "assisting" the players and should encourage all players to engage in the challenge.

53

Game Variations Suggestions

1. Use two or more teams and compare results.
2. Allow only one player to touch the spots.
3. Require five different players to enter the play area to step on or touch the NUMBERS.
4. Create other numbered patterns.
5. Use letters of the alphabet. Spell out words and sentences.

Collective Score
Team Building
Equipment:
7-15 soft objects; rings, foam/tennis balls

group juggling

7-15 Players
Upper Elementary to Adult
Play Area:
Indoor or Outdoor

To Begin

The LEADER divides the players into groups of seven to fifteen. The players are arranged in a small, close circle with all of the players facing toward the center of the circle. The LEADER should play the game and should be the player who initiates action for the game. When players understand the game, one of the players can become the new LEADER.

Next

All of the players raise one hand. The LEADER hands an object (ball, ring, bean bag, etc.) to any player in the circle that has their hand raised (except a player to the immediate right or left of them). The player who receives the object then hands it to another player across the circle from them (but not a player next to him/her). This will continue until everyone has touched the object only once.

Setup

X = Players

Third

Players take their hand down once they receive the object. The last player with the object hands it back to the LEADER (make a change in the sequence if the last player stands next to the LEADER). Each player must remember who they received the object from and who they handed it to. The LEADER will repeat the process several times so everyone remembers the handing sequence. Once the sequence is learned, the LEADER will gather 7 to 15 objects. (The more players, the more objects).

Objective

The LEADER begins handing the objects out one at a time following the handing sequence until all items are handed out. If an object is dropped, players leave it and continue to play. After awhile, the LEADER will stop the game and have the players take several steps back from the circle. The LEADER starts the game again by throwing (and not handing) the objects to the players. Players may pick up dropped items that lie close to them and continue the throwing sequence. Players should not leave the circle to pick up an object.

54

Game

Variations

Suggestions

1. Say the players name and make eye contact each time an object is handed or passed.
2. Motion can be added to this game by having the groups move as they catch and throw.

3. One group can be placed inside the circle of another group. A third group can also be added.
4. Juggle special objects: water balloons, toys, etc

Problem Solving
Team Building
Equipment:
Platform or Large Rock

onboard

7-15 Players
Middle School to Adult
Play Area:
Indoor or Outdoor

To Begin

The LEADER needs to prepare and place a platform in an open area with no obstacles surrounding it. The size and height of the platform will in part determine the challenge for the players. The platform must be sturdy and no more than two feet off the ground. Two foot by two foot, three foot by three foot or four foot by four foot platforms are easy to construct and can be used for other activities. A natural platform such as a rock can be used if it meets the recommended criteria.

Next

The entire group of players must be able to stand on the platform (not lie down on it) without anyone touching the ground. The players must be able to stabilize themselves for three to five seconds to accomplish the goal. If there are two or more platforms, the players start with the largest platform. Once they succeed, they can move to a smaller platform.

Setup

X = Players O = Leader

Platform

Rules

1. In order to be counted as being on the platform, each player must have both feet off the ground.
2. Encourage the players to "spot" each other as more players get ONBOARD.
3. When Players "fall" from the platform, they should step off rather than taking others with them.
4. The LEADER must present the challenge and then must step back and let the group decide how to accomplish the goal.
5. At a "START" command by the LEADER, the group attempts the challenge.

Leader

The LEADER needs to encourage and enforce safety procedures. It may be necessary for the LEADER to nix some of the group ideas. The LEADER must observe and not become a participant in this game. Success in this game may be determined by the number of players ONBOARD, if the group cannot accomplish the task. There are "touching" and close proximity issues for the LEADER to take into consideration.

55

Game Variations Suggestions

1. Use different platform sizes to increase or decrease the challenge.
2. Time the group making certain that safety is the highest priority.

3. Two or more groups can "race" each other if platforms are available.

Equipment:
1 Inflated Balloon per Player

Play Area:
Indoor or Outdoor

To Begin

Four or eight teams with two to five players per team will compete in an elimination tournament (Mueller Anderson - See Tournament Chapter - page 133). Once teams have been determined and each team agrees to a "team name", the LEADER places the "team name" randomly on the brackets. The LEADER will: 1) start the game, 2) add additional balloons as the game progresses, and 3) take charge of timing and running the tournament brackets.

Next

Players arrange themselves close enough to each other to interact and to work as a team. Teams should be in close proximity but maintain their own space. Before play begins, 12" balloons must be fully inflated as follows: 2 players per team = 10 balloons, 3 players per team = 15 balloons, 4 players per team = 20 balloons, and 5 players per team = 22 balloons. Each player on each team (two teams compete at one time) starts with one balloon per player. The extra balloons should be readily assessable for the LEADER.

Setup

X = Players
L = Leader

```
X          X
X          X
X          X
X          X
X          X
X          X
      L
```

Third

At a given signal from the LEADER, all players from the teams competing, toss their balloons into the air. It is the responsibility of the LEADER to monitor the action of the participants and teams. The balloons must remain in the air and not touch the floor or walls. Players may use their hands, elbows, feet, knees and head to keep the balloons airborne. Teams should develop their own strategy for keeping the balloons airborne. Teams may not intentionally interfere with their opponents. The objective of the game is for the players to keep their balloons airborne longer than their opponents.

To Play

Once a "FRENZY" starts, the LEADER adds one additional balloon for each team after 10 to 30 seconds (this depends on skill level). The LEADER continues to add additional balloons for each team simultaneously. This process continues until one team "allows" a balloon to hit the floor. Action stops at that point. All balloons are collected for the next "FRENZY" competition. The tournament brackets are updated after each "FRENZY". All teams will play the same number of games.

56

Game Variations Suggestions

1. The team must not only keep the balloons in the air but must also move them across a playing surface.
2. Large groups can play by attempting to keep all balloons airborne for as long a time as possible (usually 5-7 more balloons than number of participants). Multiple group attempts are best.

Equipment:
20'-30' Rope/Bungee Cord

Play Area:
Indoor or Outdoor

To Begin

Secure a bungee cord or a rope tightly between two objects. The height of THE FENCE will be determined by the size, age and skill level of the players. The area under THE FENCE should be free from obstacles. All of the players start the game on one side of THE FENCE with the LEADER on the other side.

Next

The goal of the game is to get all of the players from one side of THE FENCE to the other side. Once the game starts, no player can 1) touch or bump up against or 2) use foreign objects to lower or move THE FENCE. There is an "invisible" barrier beneath THE FENCE which cannot be violated by any player. The LEADER serves as a "referee".

Setup

X
X
X
X
X
X
X
X

O

O = Leader
X = Players

Third

The game starts with all players joined together. There must be constant physical connection between all participants (hands touching hands, shoulders, clothing, etc). If this connection breaks down at any juncture, the group must restart the game from the beginning. If a "restart" is necessary, the group should be encouraged to communicate with all players to determine a "better" or "different" plan.

To End

The game ends when all players have reached the opposite side of THE FENCE without: 1) any touches on THE FENCE and 2) without any disruption of the group connection. Any violation that is obvious or determined by the "referee" requires the group to restart from the beginning.

Game Variations Suggestions

1. The LEADER can time the group to see how quickly (and safely) they can complete the goal.
2. One third of the players can be blindfolded or play with eyes closed.
3. Note: The group connection rule will 1) eliminate the "body launch" technique which can result in injuries and 2) require a lower level FENCE.

Problem Solving
Team Building
Equipment:
Blindfolds/Bandanas & 15" Rope per Player

8-30 Players
Middle School to Adult
Play Area:
Indoor or Outdoor

sherpa walk

To Begin

The LEADER or LEADERS will meet prior to beginning the game to establish an obstacle course. LEADERS should be familiar with the activity. Indoor obstacles may include hallways, stairs, doors, desks, etc. Outdoor obstacles may include sidewalks, brush, branches on trees, hills, etc. Plan the obstacle course as a loop. Challenge the group but don't make it impossible.

Players will eventually connect by holding onto a 15 inch piece of rope per player or they can hold hands.

Next

Players and LEADERS should meet in a place away from the obstacle course to get organized and to receive instructions. Form equal number groups of 8-15 players. There should be one LEADER per group. Two players from each group are picked to be the SHERPAS. The SHERPAS leave the meeting area with one of the LEADERS and quickly walk through the obstacle course.

Setup

X = Players
L = Leader
S = Sherpa

Third

The players are each given blindfolds by another LEADER. Trust aspects in blindfolded activity should be discussed. The SHERPAS return and talk with their group about communication strategies while on the walk. The SHERPAS do not wear blindfolds, cannot talk and can not touch players in their group. A communication system needs to be established (whistling, hand clapping, clicking fingers, mouth sounds, etc.). Reminder: once the SHERPA WALK starts, there should be NO verbal communication unless safety is an issue.

Objective

The players are then led to the start of the obstacle course where they quickly put on their blindfolds. If there is more than one group, allow time for each group to get started. Another possibility is to start two groups at once in opposite directions. LEADER/s will accompany each group to provide observations at the end of the activity. Groups move with caution. Players in the groups can assist each other by "touching" teammates.
LEADERS may have to step in to spot at certain places on the course.

58

Game
Variations
Suggestions

1. Assure players that LEADERS will step into the activity if there are any unsafe situations.

2. It is essential to talk about the

activity at its conclusion. Get feedback from players, SHERPAS and the LEADERS about trust, silence, fear, etc.

Competitive Game
Team Building
Equipment:
1 Chair per Player

new musical chairs

10-20 Players
Lower Elementary to Adult
Play Area:
Indoor or Outdoor

To Begin

The LEADER of the game arranges chairs in a circular or rectangular pattern. The chairs should be very close together with no or few gaps. The chairs must be accessible for all players who will move clockwise around the chairs when the game begins. Two sets of chairs should be arranged: 1) a small circle with two chairs and 2) a large circle with three chairs less than the total number of players.

Next

All of the players arrange themselves a set distance from the chairs in the large circle. Cones or markers can be used to keep the distance consistent. NOTE: Too much of a distance can result in safety issues. The LEADER begins the game by playing music. The players rotate around the circle and the chairs in a clockwise path. At some point, the LEADER stops the music. The players must locate an empty chair and sit in the chair before other players. Three players will not be seated at the end of the first round.

Setup

X = Players   L = Chairs

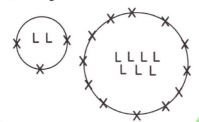

Third

The three players who did not locate a chair after the first round move to the smaller circle of chairs. The LEADER then removes two chairs from the larger circle. When the music starts, players will rotate clockwise around the large circle of chairs and around the small circle of chairs. When the music stops, the players from both circles attempt to sit in a vacant chair in their circle.

To End

The two players from the larger circle who have not found a chair then move to the smaller circle. The two players from the smaller circle who have found a chair then move to the larger circle. Action continues. The game ends after a few more rotations. At that point, each player sitting reaches below the chair they are sitting on. Prizes or awards can be adhered to the bottom of the chairs.

59

Game Variations Suggestions

1. The game can be played without prizes or rewards.
2. Change the movement around the circles: running, skipping, dancing, walk backward, etc.

3. Set a time limit for the game before starting play.

4. Substitute chants or cheers for the music.

Problem Solving
Team Building
Equipment:
1" Tubular Webbing (12'-15')

racoon circles

10-80 Players
Upper Elementary to Adult
Play Area:
Indoor or Outdoor

To Begin

Standing in a circle, ten to fourteen players hold on to the webbing, which has been joined with a water knot (overhand follow through). Each player moves their feet slightly to the center of the circle while leaning back. Players attempt to maintain their balance. (Eyes can be closed to encourage connection and trust). Once accomplished, players can attempt balance by using one hand (and then the other, one foot (and then the other), or they can turn around backward with hands on the webbing and lean forward.

Next

Still standing in the circle holding onto the webbing, each player leans backwards and slowly sinks to the ground where they sit. At another signal, each player leans backwards and stands up. Repeat a couple of times. Then have each team, while standing, agree on a sound that they will make when they sit and another sound when they stand. Each team can practice. If there is more than one team, each team can demonstrate to the other teams their sounds and movement.

# Setup
X= Players
L= Leader

L

Third

Each group ties a knot in the middle of the RACCOON CIRCLE to form two equal loops. Players hold hands with one of the "new" webbing circles around the arm of one person. The task is to pass the loop completely around the circle without disconnecting hands. Teams can "race" each other. A more complex task is the figure eight pass. Make sure the loops are equal in size before being placed over one player's arm. One loop will be passed to the right and the other to the left. Teams can "race" each other or they can be timed.

Finally

Players stand inside the RACCOON CIRCLE with the webbing about waist high. One or two players can stand on the outside to direct the movement. The task is for everyone in the group to move safely and efficiently from one place to another without touching the webbing with their hands. Possible commands: "Take five steps forward", "Turn in a complete circle", "Walk from one room to another". It is possible to set up an obstacle course for each team to complete.

60

Game

Variations

Suggestions

1. The RACCOON CIRCLE can be twisted into a series of four small circles so a web bed is formed. A player can lay on the bed with one Player responsible to safely hold his/

her head. The team can lift, lower and rock the player. More responsible groups can move players from one place to another in a relay race. Monitor for safety.

all catch and up chuck

Equipment:
1 Styrofoam Ball per Player

Play Area:
Indoor or Outdoor

To Begin

All of the players arrange themselves randomly in the play area (no particular formation). Players need to be close enough to each other to interact and to work as a team. A LEADER needs to be present to start the action and to have control of the Styrofoam balls, which should total the same amount as the number of players.

Next

1. The players may not catch the same ball that they throw into the air.

2. All players must catch a ball thrown by another player.

3. All balls must be thrown approximately 10 feet into the air.

4. If a ball touches the floor or ground, action stops and play starts over.

Setup

X = Players   XX = IT

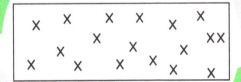

Third

The Leader will start the action by giving a ball to one of the players. At a given signal by the LEADER, the first player will toss their ball into the air. Another player in the group must then catch the ball before the ball hits the ground or the floor. If the first ball is caught, a second player is given a ball and at the given signal, two balls are thrown into the air. If both balls are caught, a third ball is entered into the action. The objective of this game is to have every player throw a ball into the air and to have every ball caught.

Rules

Another way to play this game is to provide every player with a Styrofoam ball at the start of the game. At a given signal from the LEADER, all players will throw their ball into the air. The LEADER will keep track of how many balls are caught. The objective of this game is to catch as many balls as possible with ten to twenty attempts.

Game Variations Suggestions

1. Change equipment: Balloons, Whiffle Balls, Water Balloons, Frisbees, Rubber Chickens, Bean Bags, Rubber Rings, etc.
2. Include movement: Turn in a circle before catching, kneel down before catching, etc.
3. Play the game using a Competitive Format. Two teams play until one team drops a ball.

Problem Solving
Team Building
Equipment:
None

tiny teachings

10-20 Players
High School to Adult
Play Area:
Indoor or Outdoor

To Begin

Players begin the game by arranging themselves in a circle facing toward the center. Each player should stand next to a partner. The LEADER also joins the circle. If there is an odd number, the LEADER can pair up with that player. Although no equipment is necessary, it can be helpful to have an assortment of gear available (foam balls, Frisbees, bean bags, hula hoops, cones, balloons, etc).

Next

The LEADER explains that each partner group will be provided ten minutes to leave the circle area and to scatter throughout the space available away from other groups. Each player from each group will have five minutes to share and teach their partner something that they know well. At the end of five minutes, their partner will have the same task, share and teach their partner something that they know well. At the conclusion of the TINY TEACH-INGS, each partner should be able to teach what they have learned to the entire group.

Setup

X = Players
O = Leader

Third

Players return to the circle. The LEADER asks for volunteers to teach to the entire group what they have learned (with no or little help from their partners). It is best to ask for volunteers. The LEADER encourages as many players to teach as possible. With smaller groups, each player can teach what they have learned. The LEADER should also have observed the TINY TEACHINGS and should attempt to have the "special" leanings presented. It can be intimidating for players to have to teach. It may be prudent to provide examples if players have no idea what to share.

Examples

The LEADER may want to share a list of possible TINY TEACHING activities (if player are stuck):

Learn a song or poem, make a special noise, perform a stunt or a fitness move, count to ten in a foreign language, yodel, perform a cheer, explain how to collect items, learn a dance step, juggle, make a paper airplane, take a great photo, learn a magic trick, and many more.

Game Variations Suggestions

1. Players should pick partners that they do not already know.
2. Adult and youth partnerships can be powerful. Have the youth teach first.
3. Play with partners teaching partners.
4. It's all right if a partner "messes up" the lesson that was just learned. LEADERS should process

Guessing Game
Team Building

Equipment:
4-8 Cones for Boundaries

fish gobbler

12-40 Players
Lower Elementary to Adult

Play Area:
Indoor or Outdoor

To Begin

All players line up behind one of the two goal lines. The first FISH GOBBLER should be the LEADER. The GOBBLER must be familiar with the ACTIONS and COMMANDS used in the game. The GOBBLER takes a position near the center of the four goal lines and faces the players (FISH). When the action starts, the GOBBLER moves around the play area with arms outstretched like a big animal, swimming towards the FISH. The GOBBLER moves very slowly and makes weird noises.

Next

The GOBBLER yells out COMMANDS for the FISH to follow. It is important for the LEADER to explain each of the COMMMANDS and to demonstrate the appropriate ACTIONS before the game begins. The GOBBLER tells players they will be sent to the FISH MARKET and become FILLLETS if they don't obey the COMMANDS. Also if a FISH gets tagged by the GOBBLER, they too become a FILLET and must stay in the MARKET until they are rescued. The goals and special areas need to be clearly marked and pointed out to the players.

Setup

X = Players
XX = IT

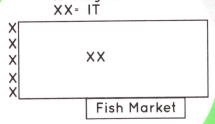

XX

Fish Market

Third

These are the COMMANDS and ACTIONS that the FISH must obey.

SHIP: FISH run to safety behind the GOAL LINE that the GOBBLER points to.
SHORE: FISH run to safety behind the GOAL LINE opposite the one the GOBBLER points to.
RESCUE: This command gives FISH five seconds to rescue any FILLETS trapped at the MARKET. While the GOBBLER counts to five, four FISH can join hands around a FILLET and escort them to safety.

Commands

SARDINES: FISH run to the center and stand as close together as possible.

FISHERMAN ALL: FISH sit on another FISH'S knee and pretends to ...fish!

It is important to introduce the commands one at a time and to provide time for the players to practice each command. The game should begin in slow motion with the first LEADER (the GOBBLER) being very familiar with the game and the game commands.

Game Variations Suggestions

1. More possible commands:
CRABS: FISH back up to a partner, bend at the waist and reach between their legs to grab their partner's hands.

FISHNET: FISH form small circles (SCHOOLS), reach into the center and grab the hands of one other player.

Competitive Game
Relay Game
Equipment:
4'-6' Noodle per Team

jack be nimble relay

12-60 Players
Upper Elementary to Adult
Play Area:
Indoor or Outdoor

To Begin

Teams with even numbers are formed. The play area should have a start line and an end line clearly marked with space to maneuver. Each team lines up in a single file line behind the start line. Each team is given a 4-6 foot Noodle or pole.

Next

The LEADER gives the start command. The first player in each line of each team races with the Noodle in hand through the play area and past the end line. At that point, one end of the Noodle is placed on the ground and the other end is held against the forehead. Each player must rotate completely in one circle. After the circle, the player races back to their team carrying the Noodle.

Setup

X = Players

End Line	Start Line
	XXXXX
	XXXXX
	XXXXX
	XXXXX
30 to 60 Feet	XXXXX

Third

When a player returns, the next player in line grabs one end of the Noodle while the runner grabs the other end. These two players lower the Noodle and sweep down their team as all of the players jump over the passing Noodle. Once at the end, the Noodle is reversed and all of the players again jump over the returning Noodle.

To End

When the Noodle finally gets to the front of the line, the second player races with the Noodle to the end line and back repeating the spin move and the sweep move with the third player. In the mean time the first player takes a position at the end of the line. The game is over when all players have had a chance to run, spin and sweep. The first team to complete the game is the winner.

64

Game
Variations
Suggestions

1. The players need to be careful when sweeping so that a teammate doesn't step on the Noodle and hurt their fingers. The Noodle can be held lightly with the thumb and forefinger.
2. Be careful with the spin move. Too many spins result in a dizzy sensation.
3. Play with partners locking arms

Tag Game
Competitive Game
Equipment: 1 Foam Ball
4 Cones for Boundaries

needle and thread tag

12-16 Players
Upper Elementary to Adult
Play Area:
Indoor or Outdoor

To Begin

Players form a circle with all players facing inward. The LEADER is a member of the circle and plays the game. Players must be close enough together to hold hands but far enough apart for a player to move between them. Two players of equal athletic ability volunteer to start the game as the IT and the RUNNER. The RUNNER starts the game in the center of the circle. The IT holds a foam ball and starts the game outside the circle. Markers may be set up to keep the players from running too far away from the circle.

Next

The LEADER demonstrates the game in slow motion. At a START command, the IT attempts to tag the RUNNER with the foam ball. The Runner attempts to avoid being tagged. The IT will start by entering the inner circle. The gap where the IT passed is immediately closed by the players on each side who quickly join hands. The RUNNER will move through an open gap, which will immediately close. The IT and RUNNER continue a tag game while the players close all of the gaps. The RUNNER and IT cannot run under a closed gap.

Setup

X = Players
R = Runner
IT = IT

X   X   X
X   X
X   X
X   IT
X
X   X
                R
X   X
X   X
X   X   X

Third

If and when the IT tags the RUNNER, The RUNNER becomes the new IT. The previous IT hands the ball to the new IT. The new IT must spin in a circle and then chase the new RUNNER. The goal of the game is for the circle to be completely closed with the RUNNER on the inside or outside of the circle and the IT on the other side. The ideal outcome is for the RUNNER to end up safe.

To End

The game ends when the entire circle is closed. There are three outcomes: 1) both the IT and RUNNER are inside the circle, 2) both the IT and RUNNER are outside the circle, or 3) the game goal has been reached. At the conclusion of the first game, a second game begins with two new players of equal athletic ability. Play continues until everyone has had a turn to play.

65

Game Variations Suggestions

1. With very large numbers, the game can be played with partners locking arms.
2. Movement can be changed: skipping, walking backward, etc.

3. Play until the RUNNER has been safe five to ten times (outcome three).

Relay Game
Team Building

Equipment:
None

12-30 Players
Middle School to Adult

Play Area:
Indoor or Outdoor

laughing logs

To Begin

All of the players stand in a single file line with big, small, male and female players evenly distributed throughout the line-up. A grassy, carpeted or matted area is best for this game. If outside, a grassy area with a slight downhill is preferred.

Next

All of the players lay on their stomachs so they are side-by-side and facing in the same direction. It is very important that all players lay as closely together as possible. There should not be any spaces between players. Player's arms and shoulders should be as far forward (bracing position) as possible but should remain on the ground.

Setup
X = Players
O = Leader

O x x x x x x x x x x x x

Third

The object of the game is for all of the players to roll, one at a time to the end of the line. When a player gets to the end of the line, they again lay on the ground as close as possible to the person next to them. The LEADER begins the game at the front of the line by rolling over the person next to them, and continues rolling until they reach the end of the line of LAUGHING LOGS. The LEADER takes the position as the new end of the line by laying on the ground, tightly positioned against the person next to them.

Rules

As soon as the LEADER rolls over the second player, the second player starts rolling down the line. When the second player has rolled over the third player, the third player starts rolling down the line. Action continues until all of the players have rolled completely over the other LAUGHING LOGS. When players are rolling, they must be careful not to roll too fast and to be considerate of the person in front of them. Players should also be careful with their elbows when rolling.

66

Game Variations Suggestions

1. Have players roll one direction and then roll back in the opposite direction.

2. Two teams may wish to race their LAUGHING LOGS to the end of the line.

3. Teams may want to divide by height and weight.

4. Note: If the lines are too long, the act of rolling over multiple times can make people dizzy.

Problem Solving
Collective Score
Equipment:
None

popsicle push-ups

12-40 Players
Middle School to Adult
Play Area:
Indoor or Outdoor

To Begin

This game is a variation of the standard one person push-up. It is important that the players in this game are capable of completing a push-up. The LEADER has the choice of 1) just explaining the game and the objective of the game or 2) explaining the game and providing a demonstration.

Next

At the conclusion of the game, all of the players must be able to be in a push-up position with only their hands touching the ground. In essence, they create a large group POPSICLE PUSH-UP.

Setup

Third

The easiest way to teach the game is to start doing a four player push-up. The first player lies down on his/her stomach. The second player lies down perpendicular to the first, with feet and ankles over the lower back of the first player. The third and fourth players do the same thing, with the first player's feet over the lower back of the fourth player so that all of the torsos form a square.

Challenge

The challenge is to have all four players do a push-up at the same time and to hold it for five seconds. When this is accomplished, the goal is to add players until the entire group is in the push-up position for five or more seconds.

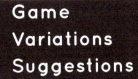

67

Game Variations Suggestions

1. It may be necessary to move players around the play area so that the feet on thier backs is possible to lift.

2. A few players can assist by providing support to "struggling" players.

3. The LEADER may want to process the outcome of the game.

Competitive Game
Guessing Game
Equipment: 1 Object and Dice
4 Cones for Boundaries

impulse

14-40 Players
Upper Elementary to Adult
Play Area:
Indoor or Outdoor

To Begin

Players form equal groups of seven to twenty players. Groups arrange themselves close together in single file lines. The lines should face each other with the LEADER positioned at the far end of the lines. The players in each line sit close enough to each other so that they are able to place their hands behind their backs and hold onto the player's hands immediately next to them. Boundary markers are then placed at the front and rear of the lines. Players must remain in the boundary lines during the game.

Next

The only players not holding both hands of another player will be the front and rear players from both teams. An object (ball, ring, Frisbee, beanbag, etc.) is placed 10 - 20 feet from the far end of the lines (away from the LEADER). The LEADER requires all of the players on both teams to turn their heads to face the object except the front two players. The front two players turn their heads to face the LEADER.

Setup

X = Players
O = Leader

● Object | X X X X X X X
| X X X X X X X O

Third

This is a non-verbal game (no talking). The LEADER shakes the dice and lets the dice roll on the ground so that the first two players have an equal opportunity to view the numbers. The front two players must quickly add up the totals of the dice and decide if the total is an "even" number or an "odd" number. If the total number is an even number, the front player squeezes the hand of the player next to them. That player then squeezes the hand of the player next to them. This continues to the end of the team's line. No talking!

Rules

The last person in line must then cross their goal line and attempt to grab the object before the other team's last player grabs the object. If successful, the player moves to the front of the line and becomes the start for the new IMPULSE. The team not grabbing the object stays in place. If an IMPULSE is passed to the end of the line on an "odd" number, the team that makes the mistake must move in the opposite direction. The object of the game is for everyone on a team to grab the object and to rotate back to their starting place.

Game Variations Suggestions

1. For older groups, use four, six or eight dice.
2. Place the object further away from the end line to require more action.

3. Time may be a factor with large groups. Consider a time limit.

4. Use coins or playing cards instead of dice.

Name Game
Team Building
Equipment:
None

people to people

15-41 Players
Lower Elementary to Adult
Play Area:
Indoor or Outdoor

To Begin

There must be an odd number of players to play this game. All of the players arrange themselves around a circle and next to a partner. The player without a partner becomes the first IT and stands in the middle of the circle. The IT tells all of the players their name. The players respond by saying loudly, "Hi _____!" Partners should introduce themselves to each other and to each new partner they meet during the game. The LEADER should play the game if there is a need for an odd number of players.

Next

The game begins when the LEADER loudly yelling out certain commands. Each set of partners will perform the commands together. The commands should start off easy and get more difficult. The LEADER will provide each set of commands for each round. Commands can be written down and should be practiced prior to playing the game.

Setup
X = Players
L = Leader
IT = IT

Third

The partners continue to follow the commands (3 to 4 commands work best) until the LEADER loudly yells, "PEOPLE TO PEOPLE!" This is the signal for everyone to let go of their partner, run into the middle of the circle and find a new partner by grabbing on to the new partner's hands. The IT will also try to find a partner. The new partners will then find a place around the circle. The player left without a partner is the new IT. The game then continues with the IT introduction and with the LEADER yelling out new commands.

Commands

1.
(a) Face your partner and hold both of their hands.
(b) Touch your partner's knees with your knees.
(c) Lean backwards.
(d) "PEOPLE TO PEOPLE!"
2.
(a) Stand back to back and lock arms.
(b) Touch the back of your heads.
(c) Stand on your left feet only.
(d) "PEOPLE TO PEOPLE!"

69

Tag Game
Collective Score

queen bee tag

Equipment: 3 Large Foam Balls
4 Cones for Boundaries

15-30 Players
Upper Elementary to Adult
Play Area:
Indoor with 2 Walls

To Begin

This game plays best in the corner of a room. One player is selected to be the QUEEN BEE. Two to three players are chosen to be CHASERS. The other players are the DRONES. The DRONES scatter freely throughout the HIVE (play area). The QUEEN stands inside the HIVE with the foam ball in hand. The foam ball may be thrown at DRONES so it should be soft and yet should be able to be thrown accurately in the play area. The CHASERS should position themselves outside the play area to assist with retrieving the ball if it goes out of bounds.

Next

The Queen has two possible ways to tag a DRONE. The Queen can run and touch a DRONE with the ball or the QUEEN can throw the ball at a DRONE. If the ball is thrown out of bounds, one of the CHASERS will toss a second ball to the QUEEN and then retrieve the first ball so that action is continuous.

Setup

X = Drones   O = Chasers
XX = Queen Bee

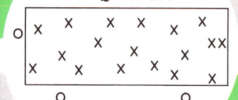

Third

When a DRONE is tagged or touched with the ball, they must stop and drop to their knees at that spot. The DRONE then becomes a WORKER and will raise both hands over their head. The QUEEN now has a third way to catch DRONES. The QUEEN can throw the ball to a WORKER who can then attempt to hit a DRONE or the WORKER can throw to other WORKER BEES. The WORKERS cannot move from the spot at which they were tagged or touched.

Strategies

Teamwork is the easiest way to tag or touch a DRONE. The WORKERS should cooperate with the QUEEN to capture all of the DRONES. The last DRONE to be touched or tagged becomes the QUEEN BEE for the next game. DRONES that leave the HIVE must kneel and become WORKERS.

70

Game Variations Suggestions

1. To encourage teamwork, each game can be timed to see how quickly all of the DRONES can be eliminated.

2. With a large number of players

two QUEENS can be selected to start the game.

3. The size of the play area may need to be adjusted to keep the flow of the game positive.

swat

Equipment:
Frisbee & 2' Noodle/Rolled Up Newspaper

Play Area:
Indoor or Outdoor

To Begin

A Frisbee (or a square base) and a two foot Noodle or rolled up newspaper are required for this game. If using newspaper, the newspaper should be rolled up "lengthwise" (longer than shorter). The Noodle or paper becomes the SWAT TOOL. The "SWAT TOOL" should have some flex and be able to bend. Players form a large circle facing toward the center about shoulder to arms length apart.

Next

The LEADER places the Frisbee in the center of the circle with the rounded side down. The LEADER begins the game as the SWATTER by walking around the inside of the circle close to the players with the "SWAT TOOL" in hand. At some point, the SWATTER swings the "SWAT TOOL" at a player and hits them on the thigh or lower leg. The SWATTER immediately runs to the center of the circle toward the upside down Frisbee.

Setup

X = Players
O = Swatter
● Frisbee

Third

The player "swatted" also runs towards the center of the circle. The SWATTER must place the "SWAT TOOL" on the top of the upside down Frisbee and run as fast as possible through the opening in the circle where the swatted player was positioned. The SWATTER continues around the outside of the circle and returns to the position vacated by the player swatted. The swatted player grabs the "SWAT TOOL" and chases the SWATTER through the opening and around the circle in an attempt to "SWAT" the SWATTER.

Rules

1. If the "SWAT TOOL" rolls off the Frisbee, the swatted player can return to the circle and does not have to chase the SWATTER (unless that player chooses to chase).
2. If the SWATTER gets "Swatted" by the chaser, the SWATTER remains the LEADER
3. If the swatted player cannot swat the SWATTER, they become the new LEADER
4. Once a player has been "Swatted" or has been a SWATTER, they kneel down and cheer for other players until everyone has had a turn.

Game Variations Suggestions

1. The "SWAT TOOL "can be hurtful if using a newspaper that it is bound too tightly together.
2. If a "SWATTER" chooses not to be a SWATTER (gets tired), any other player can be handed the "SWAT TOOL" and becomes the SWATTER.
3. Remind players to be careful and aware of how hard they "swat" other players.

Problem Solving
Tag Game
Equipment:
6 Cones for Boundaries

16-40 Players
Upper Elementary to Adult
Play Area:
Indoor or Outdoor

lemonade

To Begin

Divide the players into two equal teams. Each team lines up on opposite sides of their Goal Line. Players should be a shoulder length apart. One team starts the game by being the ACTORS. The other team will be the GUESSERS. The ACTORS select a city and an occupation from that city.

The LEADER should conduct a walk through demonstration before actually playing the game. A good example: "INDIANAPOLIS" and "RACE CAR DRIVERS"

Next

The ACTORS line up on their goal line, take three giant steps toward the center line and yell (as they step), "HERE WE COME!" The GUESSERS also line up on their goal line, take three giant steps toward the center line and reply, "WHERE `YA FROM?" (Each team takes three giant steps with each and every response). The ACTORS yell, "INDIANAPOLIS!" The GUESSERS ask, "WHAT'S YOUR TRADE? "The ACTORS reply, "LEMONADE!" The GUESSERS yell, "WELL SHOW US SOME IF YOU'RE NOT AFRAID!"

Setup

X = Players

```
        Goal Line
      XXXXXXXX
       Center Line
      XXXXXXXX
        Goal Line
```
30 to 60 Feet

30 to 100 Feet

Third

The ACTORS and the GUESSERS should be face to face near the centerline after all of the giant steps and responses have been completed. The ACTORS then begin to act out the TRADE. The GUESSERS attempt to figure out the ACTOR'S TRADE by loudly yelling out their guesses. The GUESSERS must guess the exact TRADE word for word.

To Play

As soon as one of the GUESSERS yells out the correct and exact TRADE, the ACTORS must turn around and run back across their goal line before being tagged by the GUESSERS. If an ACTOR is tagged, they become a member of the other team for the next game. A GUESSER may tag more then one Actor. The role of ACTORS and GUESSERS switches after each round. A game LEADER may want to prepare five to ten city and trade ideas in advance and share them, one at a time, with each new set of ACTORS.

Game Variations Suggestions

1. The LEADER should spend time looking for interesting, but not common trades (jobs) that can be matched to various cities, i.e., Omaha Meat Cutters or Fairbanks Dog Sledders.
2. It is important for the LEADER to emphasize that the GUESSERS must yell out their guesses

Relay Game
Collective Score
Equipment:
None

skin the snake

16-50 Players
Middle School to Adult
Play Area:
Indoor or Outdoor

To Begin

The LEADER lines up all of the players from tallest to shortest and then divides them into two equal teams. Teams form two single file lines at least ten feet apart. All players line up one behind the other facing the opposite direction of the LEADER. The LEADER needs to make sure that the play space is at least twice as long as a line of players.

Next

All players reach between their legs with their left hand and grab the right hand of the player behind them. The player in front will reach back to grab a right hand. Once the SNAKE is formed, the game can begin. At the starting signal from the LEADER, the last player in line lies down on their back. The player in front backs up straddling the player lying down and lies down right behind the first player. Players must continue to hold hands! This sequence continues as the entire team moves backward while straddling teammates.

Setup

X = Players
L = Leader

```
XX XXXXX XX XXXXX

L    ←

XX XXXXX XX XXXXX
```

Third

When the last player from a team lies down and touches their head to the ground, that player then stands (while still holding hands) and gets set to move forward (back to the Start) while pulling all other teammates to their feet. The winning team is the first team that gets all of its members standing and past the GOAL LINE while still holding hands. If hands become disconnected during the game, the team must stop and hands must be reconnected at that point before proceeding.

Hints

Players should play with their shoes off.

When the line is moving backward, players should bunch together.

Players should lie down as close as they can to the player in front of them and they should tuck their feet to that person's side, toes pointed in.

The last player to lay down should be fast, agile and have a very firm grip.

73

Game Variations Suggestions

1. Safety consideration: As players back up, they need to be especially careful where they step.
2. A quick practice session with three players per group can help prepare each team.
3. Play the game with only one line. The group can be timed and penalty time can be charged for each time that hands break.

snake pit

Equipment: 2 Cans with Pebbles Inside
2' Noodle/Rolled Up Newspaper

Play Area:
Indoor or Outdoor

To Begin

All of the players form a large circle and face the center. One player is selected to be the RATTLER and another player is chosen to be the MONGOOSE. The remaining players are the SNAKE TRAINERS and they form the boundary of the SNAKE PIT. The boundary is formed by the players standing shoulder width apart (or arms length). The MONGOOSE and the RATTLER stand in the center of the PIT. The RATTLER shakes the rattle and the MONGOOSE slaps the Noodle or rolled up paper in their open hand.

Next

The game begins with the MONGOOSE trying to tag or poke the RATTLER, but it is "dark" down in the PIT and the MONGOOSE can't see (his/her eyes are closed or blindfolded)! The MONGOOSE slaps the Noodle or paper in his/her hand making a noise that scares the RATTLER. The RATTLER shakes his/her rattle every time the MONGOOSE slaps the NOODLE OR rolled up paper hoping to frighten away the MONGOOSE.

Setup

X X
X   X
X   X
    X= Players
    M= Mongoose
    S= Rattler
X   X
    M   R
X   X
X   X
X X

Third

The MONGOOSE listens for the rattle and tries to tag the RATTLER by poking (NOT swatting) him/her with the Noodle or rolled up newspaper. The TRAINERS help to keep the MONGOOSE and the RATTLER in the PIT by making a hissing noise. The MONGOOSE has 30 seconds to tag the RATTLER. If the MONGOOSE tags or pokes the RATTLER, both players return to the edge of the circle. If the RATTLER does not get tagged in 30 seconds, both players return to the edge of the circle.

Hints

When the MONGOOSE and the RATTLER return to the edge of the circle, they choose two of the TRAINERS standing around the circle to take their place by handing them their noisemakers or poking device and blindfold. The old MONGOOSE and RATTLER kneel on the edge of the circle (so everyone knows they've had a chance to play) and join the other TRAINERS, hissing at the new MONGOOSE and RATTLER. The game continues until everyone has been either a MONGOOSE or a RATTLER.

Game Variations Suggestions

1. Noise makers must be loud. Be creative with other possibilities.

2. If there's a large number of participants, two players can be se-

lected to be RATTLERS for each game. The MONGOOSE will then attempt to tag or poke each of the RATTLERS in the 30-second time period.

alligator

Equipment:
Large Blanket/Tarp/Parachute

Play Area:
Indoor or Outdoor

To Begin

All of the players form a large circle around a "Game" parachute. Players face toward the center. A LEADER takes a position on the circle among the other players. One (or two) players are selected to be ALLIGATORS. Four (or five) players are selected to be LIFE GUARDS.

Next

All of the remaining players sit with their legs forward under the parachute while holding it waist high and taut. The players should not be able to see under the parachute. The ALLIGATORS begin the game underneath the parachute. The LIFE GUARDS arrange themselves around the outside of the parachute.

Setup

X = Players
O = Leader
LG = Lifegaurd
GAT = Alligator

Third

Players create small waves with the parachute to simulate a lake or water. At a signal from the LEADER, the game begins. Players who do not wish to be captured by an ALLIGATOR can sit with legs crossed. If a Player is saved by a LIFE GUARD, they continue play by re-taking the starting position under the again. Once a player is captured (dragged totally under the "water"), they also become ALLIGATORS. Encourage the players to scream for help.

Objective

When action begins, the ALLIGATORS move under the parachute and grab hold of any player's feet in an attempt to pull them totally under. When a player is grabbed by an ALLIGATOR, they call for help from a LIFE GUARD. A LIFE GUARD (or one or more of them) can rush to the aid of a player and attempt to save them by pulling them back to safety. The objective of the game is for all of the players to be captured by the ALLIGATORS.

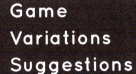

75

Game Variations Suggestions

1. A soft matted or grassy surface is recommended.
2. Safety: ALLIGATORS must be careful not to be too rough.
3. Variation: Once a player is dragged under the "water", they replace the ALLIGATOR and the ALLIGATOR becomes a player.

Problem Solving
Team Building
Equipment:
24'-30' Parachute/Tarp

20-30 Players
Lower Elementary to Adult
Play Area:
Indoor or Outdoor

big wind blows

To Begin

All of the players form a large circle around a "Game" parachute. Players face toward the center. A LEADER takes a position on the circle among the other players. All of the Players grab hold of the parachute. If there are no handles, players may roll the edges of the parachute a couple of times for better grip.

Next

At the START command by the LEADER, all of the players slowly lift the parachute up over their heads to form a billowing cloud. When the parachute returns to the ground, a couple more clouds are formed. It's important to let the parachute return with as little downward effort as possible. Once this technique is completed, the LEADER stops the action and has all of the players count off: "Apple, Orange, Banana" or some other form of organization (besides numbers).

Setup

X = Players
O = Leader

Third

Each player must remember their action word ("Apple, Orange, or Banana"). The LEADER starts the game by having all of the players slowly lift the parachute to make the billowing cloud. As soon as the parachute begins to rise, the LEADER calls out one of the action words. If the LEADER yells out "APPLES", all of the APPLES must let go of the parachute and cross under the cloud in an attempt to get to the other side. (It doesn't matter where players end up). The LEADER then calls out another action word or two words at once.

To Play

Play continues until all players have had a couple of turns. The LEADER stops play and informs the players that he/she will yell out statements and if the statement applies to any player in the game, they must let go of the parachute and cross under the cloud in an attempt to get to the other side. Examples of Statements: "Everyone wearing something green or everyone with a pet or everyone wearing jeans or everyone who is the oldest in their family." The possibilities are endless.

76

Game

Variations

Suggestions

1. There are many possible variations for this game. The Leader may want to finish the game by yelling out a statement that results in everyone letting go of the parachute at the same time. Example: "Everyone who goes to school or everyone who wears shoes."

Equipment:
24'-30' Parachute/Tarp

Play Area:
Indoor or Outdoor

To Begin

All of the players form a large circle around a "Game" parachute. Players face toward the center. A LEADER takes a position on the circle among the other players. All of the players grab hold of the parachute. If there are no handles, players may roll the edges of the parachute a couple of times for better grip.

Next

The LEADER selects three MICE and two CATS. The MICE crawl under the parachute in an attempt to hide from the CATS. The CATS start the game outside of the players and the parachute. The CATS should play with their shoes off. The game begins with all of the players kneeling or squatting while holding the parachute thigh high.

Setup
X = Players
O = Leader
M = Mice
C = Cats

Third

The LEADER yells out, "START". Each CATS attempt to catch a MOUSE. In order to catch a MOUSE, the CATS must pin the MOUSE down so it cannot escape. The MICE can move around under the parachute to avoid being caught. Play continues until both CATS have caught a MOUSE. (One MOUSE remains safe). MICE must remain under the parachute.

Rules

At a "ready" signal from the LEADER, the CATS carefully walk on top of the parachute and take a kneeling position. The MICE are hiding below. The object of the game is for the CATS to catch the MICE. Once the MICE and the CATS are in place, the players shake the parachute up and down to create waves and confusion. The players can also yell out to the CATS to help them or to confuse them.

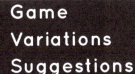

77

Game Variations Suggestions

1. A soft matted or grassy surface is recommended.
2. Change the name of the game: Fox and Hounds, Wolves and Sheep or Zombies and Kids.
3. The LEADER may want to pick CATS and MICE. The game can be more fun if the MICE are large and the CATS are smaller.

Tag Game
Team Building
Equipment:
24'-30' Parachute/Tarp

20-30 Players
Lower Elementary to Adult
Play Area:
Indoor or Outdoor

shark

To Begin

All of the players form a large circle around a "Game" parachute. Players face toward the center. A LEADER takes a position on the circle among the other players. All of the players grab hold of the parachute and hold it waist high and taut. They should not be able to see under the parachute. {The LEADER can explain the game by using the "Jaws" metaphor}.

Next

The LEADER becomes the first SHARK. The parachute becomes the ocean. The players become swimmers at the beach who are standing in shallow water in the ocean. The SHARK goes under the parachute and places both hands together over his/her head (looks like a fin).

Setup

X= Players
O= Leader

Third

Players create small waves with the parachute to simulate the ocean and begin the game by loudly humming the soundtrack from JAWS; "Dah-dum, dah-dum, dah-dum." The SHARK circles under the parachute with his/her fin in direct contact with the parachute, so the players can see the SHARK coming. At any point the SHARK can reach out and grab a payer by the lower leg. When a player is grabbed by the SHARK, they must loudly scream, "SHARK"! Note: Players should not be grabbed so they lose their balance.

To Play

1. As soon as the SHARK grabs a victim and the victim yells, "SHARK", the victim becomes the new SHARK. The game continues.

2. As soon as the SHARK grabs a victim and the victim yells, "SHARK", the victim also becomes a SHARK and both SHARKS continue to move around under the ocean selecting victims until all players have been grabbed by the SHARKS.

78

Game

Variations

Suggestions

1. A soft matted or grassy surface is recommended.
2. Much of the fun for this game can be accomplished by the LEAD-ER before the game starts by having the players practice yelling "SHARK", humming the song and waving the parachute.

Problem Solving
Team Building
Equipment:
Whistle, Bell, and Horn

20-60 Players
Lower Elementary to Adult
Play Area:
Indoor or Outdoor

touch and go

To Begin

The players scatter throughout the playing area, although they should remain near other players. The LEADER should be familiar with the game and come prepared with 10 - 20 commands. The LEADER may use the Touch and Go Commands List. (See Appendix L - Page 148).

Next

The game beings with the LEADER calling out commands. Each time the LEADER changes the command, the LEADER will clap his/her hands or blow a whistle or make some other noise to get the attention of the players. The LEADER will then change the command. Each command will take fifteen to thirty seconds. The LEADER may participate in the game.

Setup

X = Players   L = Leader

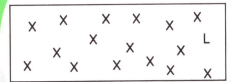

Third

This is a game about forming and reforming groups as quickly as possible. Commands change from a TOUCH (grouping) to a GO (moving as individuals). Plan this game in advance by writing down a sequence of actions. Start slow and move toward the more exciting commands. Use only 10 to 20 commands before moving to a different game.

Examples

Here is an example of a flow of commands:
"Jump up and down with your hands in the air." (a GO command)
"Touch something blue." (a TOUCH command)
"Run in place." (a GO command)
"Touch a players tennis shoe. (TOUCH)
"Skip in a small circle." (GO)
"Lock elbows with five players." (TOUCH)
"Clap your hands" (a GREAT way to end the game!)

79

Game Variations Suggestions

1. Attempt to create high energy by having the players move quickly from one command to another.
2. The last command can lead into the next game by having players form teams, i.e., "Lock elbows with ten players!" The next game begins with ten player teams.
3. Use loud fast paced music during the game.

Relay Game
Competitive Game

four square relay

20-60 Players
Upper Elementary to Adult

Equipment: 4 Balloons or Bean Bags
1 Sturdy Chair per Player + 1 Extra

Play Area:
Indoor or Outdoor

To Begin

One sturdy chair (with no arm rests) per player and one additional chair is required. The LEADER arranges all of the chairs in a "perfect" square facing an empty chair in the center. Chairs should be close together (touching if possible). There should be space at each of the four corners for players to enter the play area and to separate each team. Players enter the play area and sit on a chair facing toward the center. . All chairs should be filled except the one in the middle. Each set of players in a row of chairs becomes a team.

Next

The player on each team to the far left receives an inflated balloon. At the start command from the LEADER, the balloons are handed to each player in the line one at a time until the balloon reaches the end of the line (on the right). This player, with the balloon in hand, gets up and races clockwise around outside of all of the chairs and all of the teams. While the player is running around the outside, all of the teammates move one chair to their right so the chair that the runner returns to is vacant.

Setup

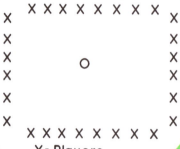

X= Players
O= Empty Chair

Third

When a players returns to their line, they begin passing the balloon to the end of the line. This pattern is repeated until every team member has run clockwise around the outside of all of the chairs and has returned to the original starting order. The first team to finish is the winning team. It is good to play this game twice (or more) to allow teams to develop a strategy.

Rules

No tossing the balloon. All players must touch it and pass it.

Players cannot interfere with other teams by grabbing or holding onto other players.

Variation: Same game except the players run clockwise around a chair that is placed in the center of all of the FOUR SQUARE chairs.

80

Game
Variations
Suggestions

1. Two or three teams can play when number are small by setting up a three sided formation.
2. Chairs can take a beating. Sturdy chairs are best.

3. Use an object to make running more difficult: a cup of water, a water balloon, a football, a lit candle (be careful), etc.

Competitive Game
Tag Game
Equipment:
6 Cones for Goal Markers

20-40 Players
Upper Elementary to Adult
Play Area:
Indoor or Outdoor

giants, wizards, and elves

To Begin

This game has three characters with three distinct actions. The GIANTS stand on their toes and stretch their bodies and hands as high as possible while looking "mean". The WIZARDS stand hunched over with their hands in front of them in a spell-casting fashion. The ELVES squat down and pull their elbows in and hands up to look very tiny. Players should practice these three actions one at a time. A good way to practice is for the LEADER to count to three and on four have all of the players become a GIANT, WIZARD and an ELF.

Next

In this game, no character is more powerful than all of the others. The strong GIANTS can easily overpower the tiny ELVES. The large number of tiny ELVES can out smart the WIZARDS. The magical WIZARDS can cast spells on the strong GIANTS.

So...GIANTS beat the ELVES, ELVES beat the WIZARDS and WIZARDS beat the GIANTS. In other words, GIANTS chase ELVES, ELVES chase WIZARDS and WIZARDS chase GIANTS.

Setup

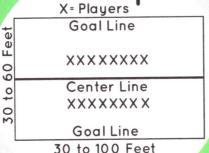

X = Players

```
        Goal Line
   
      X X X X X X X X
      ─────────────────
        Center Line
      X X X X X X X
   
        Goal Line
```
30 to 60 Feet

30 to 100 Feet

Third

Divide the players into two equal teams. Each team has a goal line. The team huddles behind the goal line and decides which of the three characters to act out. Once they have decided, both teams meet face-to-face at the centerline. Both teams, in unison, repeat the chant with appropriate actions, "GIANTS, WIZARDS, ELVES!".... "GIANTS, WIZARDS, ELVES!"..."GIANTS, WIZARDS, ELVES!" (three times). On the fourth chant, each team quickly acts out the character they picked in the huddle.

Continue

The team that is the weaker character must turn and run back across their goal line before being tagged by players from the other team. Players that get tagged become members of the team that tagged them. The "new" teams then go back behind their goal lines, pick a new character and continue to play. If the teams pick the same character, players shake hands and return to their huddles to pick another character. Play can continue until all of the players are on the same team.

81

Name Game
Team Building
Equipment: Carpet Squares
Paper or Fresbees per Player

20-50 Players
Middle School to Adult
Play Area:
Indoor or Outdoor

do you know your neighbor?

To Begin

All the players form a large circle. Players face toward the center and line up slightly more than shoulder length apart. Once lined up, each player is given a marker to stand on. The game LEADER should be the first IT. The IT stands in the middle of the circle and tells everyone his/her name. All of the players in the circle then say in unison, "HI, (IT's name)". The IT responds by saying, "HI!" All new ITS must introduce themselves to the group this way. A demonstration of the game by the LEADER is crucial.

Next

The IT tells everyone to introduce themselves to their neighbors and to remember their neighbors' first name. The IT then walks around the inside of the circle and challenges individual players. The IT will point at a player and ask, "Do you know your neighbors?" The player has three seconds to answer correctly. If the player makes a mistake, they become the new IT. If the player responds correctly, the IT will ask, "Do you like your neighbors?" The player may respond one of three ways: "YES", "NO", or "RUN FOR YOUR LIFE!".

Setup

X = Players   O = Leader

IT

Third

If the player answers, "YES", the player must add, "But I don't like people..." and end with something that describes a group of other players. Some examples include: "I don't like people... wearing hats" or "wearing something blue" or "with a belt on," etc. All players that are identified by the statement must run and find another marker on which to stand. The IT will also look for an open marker to stand on. The player left wihtout a place to stand is the new IT. Players then introduce themselves to their "new" neighbors

Last

If the player answers "NO", the players on either side of him/her must quickly change places and attempt to stand on the other person's marker. The IT will also try to stand on one of the markers left open. The player left without a marker to stand on is the new IT.

If a player answers "RUN FOR YOUR LIFE", all of the players, including the IT, scramble to find a new marker to stand on, leaving one player without a marker. That person becomes the new IT.

82

Game Variations Suggestions

1. Players may only move around the outside of the circle, instead of across the circle.
2. Players can be accountable to remember first and last names,
nicknames, hometowns, etc. of their neighbors.
3. Allow players to answer the "question" with other possibilities. Let players be creative.

Problem Solving
Competitive Game
Equipment:
None

quick line – up

20-40 Players
Middle School to Adult
Play Area:
Indoor or Outdoor

To Begin

Players form four equal groups of four to twelve players per group. Groups arrange themselves in single file lines with the players standing shoulder to shoulder in a perfect square facing inward. The LEADER stands in the center of the square.

Next

The goal of the game is for a team to get five points (one point for each winning round) before the other teams reach that number. The intensity of play can put pressure on the LEADER to make fair and firm decisions. If there are an odd number of players, the LEADER may have one or two of the "extra" players assist with determining Round winners.

Setup

```
    X X X X X X X X
X                       X
X                       X
X           L           X
X                       X
X                       X
X                       X
    X X X X X X X X
```

X = Players
L = Leader

Third

Each Round of play begins with the LEADER spinning in a circle a couple of times and coming to a complete stop facing one of the lines of players. When the LEADER stops, each team must quickly reassemble into their original order and position relative to teammates and the LEADER. The first team to accurately LINE-UP wins one point. The first team to reach five points wins the game. The LEADER can leave the square and move to another spot outside the square.

Rules

One team always faces the LEADER. The second team is always on the LEADERS right. The third team is always on the LEADERS left. The fourth team always faces the LEADERS back. Each player must remember two things: 1) his/her position in their team line and 2) the teams position in regard to the LEADER. Players may not hold onto each other when moving from one spot to another.

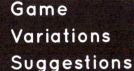

83

Game Variations Suggestions

1. Players must not intentionally hold onto or detain players from other teams during the QUICK LINE-UP.

2. Once a team wins the game, a triangle can be formed with the remaining teams. Play continues until a second team wins. Play can continue until only one-team remains

Equipment:
1 Sturdy Chair per Player

Play Area:
Indoor or Outdoor

To Begin

One sturdy chair (with no arm rests) per player and a LEADER is required. The LEADER and all of the players arrange themselves in a tight circle. All chairs face toward the center of the circle. All chairs should be touching. There can not be any gaps! The LEADER will become a player at the start of the game.

Next

All players sit on their chairs facing towards the center. The LEADER will ask the players for one volunteer (the IT) to start the WAVE. The IT stands in the center of the circle. One chair will then be vacant.

Setup

X = Players
O = Leader

X X X
X   X
X   X
X   X
X   O
X   X
X   X
X X X

Third

When the LEADER says, "Start", the IT player in the center of the group must try to sit in the empty chair. The players sitting on the chairs attempt to keep the IT from finding an empty chair. They do this by moving left or right. If the IT finds an empty chair and is able to sit in that chair, the player in the circle who allowed the IT to sit becomes the next IT. The LEADER will determine which player in the circle allowed the IT to sit. The game continues.

Challenge

The LEADER will stop the game at a "high point". The LEADER may challenge players to get up out of their chairs and move across the circle to an empty chair once the game starts again. After awhile, the LEADER will stop the game again and ask the players if everyone has run across the circle? (Some will have played it safe). Play starts again with more group movement. There is usually high action followed by a lull. The LEADER will have to determine who allowed the last player to sit. (There must always be an empty chair).

84

Game Variations Suggestions

1. The game can become quite physical. Players should be told that they should not dive or thrust themselves on to the chairs or other people.

2. Chairs can take a beating. Sturdy chairs are best.

3. Play with partners locking arms. IT will not have a partner.

Guessing Game
Team Building
Equipment:
None

20-60 Players
Middle School to Adult
Play Area:
Indoor or Outdoor

who started the stampede

To Begin

All of the players form a large circle. Players face towards the center and line up slightly more than arms length apart. One PLAYER is selected to be the IT. The IT leaves the circle and stands facing away from the circle while the remaining players select one person to be the STARTER. The STARTER is the player who leads the motions that the entire group of players will follow. The IT must not know who has been selected to be the STARTER.

Next

While the IT is still away from the circle, the STARTER will begin a motion and all of the players will begin to do the same motion. Motions can include almost anything (that is not too obvious). Examples of motions: clicking fingers, foot tapping, belly rubbing, head scratching, jumping up and down, etc. The IT then returns to the center of the circle. It is crucial that the IT remain as close to the center of the circle as possible.

Setup

X = Players IT = IT
L = Leader

L = Leader

Third

The IT tries to guess which player is the STARTER. While the IT is attempting to guess who might be the STARTER, the STARTER tries to change the motion as often as possible without being discovered by the IT. The IT makes a guess by pointing to the player suspected as being the STARTER. A STAMPEDE begins when the IT guesses incorrectly. All players (including the STARTER) take one giant step toward the center of the circle and towards the IT.

To End

The IT may make as many guesses as he/she wants. However, the object of the game is to identify the STARTER before the IT gets STAMPEDED. If the IT correctly identifies the STARTER or if the STAMPEDE overtakes the IT, a new game begins. Other players volunteer to be the STARTER and the IT.

85

Game Variations Suggestions

1. With large groups of 24 or more and with nearly equal numbers of males and females, two STARTERS and two ITS can be chosen to start the game at the same time. Male and female players play a game within a game. Males follow, guess and stampede males. Females do the same with females.

Name Game
Team Building
Equipment:
Loud Music

21-51 Players
Middle School to Adult
Play Area:
Indoor or Outdoor

fire on the mountain

To Begin

There must be an odd number of players for this game to be played. The LEADER can be considered one of the players. All of the players form a large circle. Players face toward the center and divide into pairs. One player in the pair stands in front of their partner forming two circles, one inside of the other. The inside partner remains facing the center of the circle, about shoulder width away from the next player. The outside partner turns to their left, facing in a clockwise direction and takes two or more sideway steps away from the center of the circle.

Next

The LEADER or the IT stands in the middle of the circle. The LEADER or another player will start the music (exp. YMCA, Who Let the Dogs Out, etc.). The IT needs to select a motion or dance routine that "fits" the music. The IT teaches the motion routine to the players and has them practice the motion briefly. Encourage players to be creative with the motions or dance routines. The game begins with all the players doing the routine.

Setup

X X X X
O O O O
X X
O O
X O   O X
X O

IT

X O   O X
O   O X
X O   O X
O O O X
X X X

X = Outside Circle
O = Inside Circle
IT = IT

Third

Once the music starts and the IT begins the motion, the players in the outside circle will rotate clockwise around the inside circle while performing the dance motion. The players in the inside circle remain in place while performing the dance motion. At some point, usually after 30 to 60 seconds, the IT will raise both hands high in the air. The outside circle continues rotating around the inside circle while performing the dance motion. The inside circle follows the cue of the IT and raises their hands while still performing the dance motion.

Continue

The IT then loudly yells, "FIRE ON THE MOUNTAIN!" Players from the outside circle rush to stand in front of an inside player. Inside players must remain stationary. Out side players must grab the raised hands of an inside player... not each other! The IT also tries to grab the hands of an inside player. The player without a partner is the new IT. Players from the initial inside circle take a couple of steps back to form the new outside circle and the game continues with different music.

86

Game Variations Suggestions

1. Use a chant and motion instead of using music, (clicking fingers or clapping hands while yelling "HEY, YAH! HEY, YAH!")
2. Change the motion of the out-

side circle. Run, skip, walk backward, baby steps with eyes shut.
3. Set up a circle of cones a given distance behind the inner circle for the outside circle.

Relay Game
Team Building
Equipment:
None

cookie machine

30-50 Players
Middle School to Adult
Play Area:
Indoor or Outdoor

To Begin

Players are divided into two equal lines. A good method to accomplish this is to have all of the players find a partner about the same size as themselves. Line up the partners across from each other so they are facing their partners. Players in the lines should be shoulder to shoulder. Intersperse larger and smaller partners throughout the line. A front of the line is determined. An IT is chosen to start the COOKIE MACHINE in motion.

Next

Players in each line place both hands out in front of them palm side up. Both teams move close enough to each other so that the palms of all of the players are intertwined and alternated down the entire line of the COOKIE MACHINE. Players should assume a spotting position (one foot forward and one back). Note: Watches and rings may have to be removed before the game begins. The last two players in each line assume a spotting position to assist the COOKIE off the COOKIE MACHINE once the game begins.

Setup

X = Players
S = Spotter
C = COOKIE

S X X X X X X X X X X X X X X C
X X X X X X X X X X X X X X

Third

Each player in this game has the opportunity to be the COOKIE. The first COOKIE stands facing the front of the line. Arms should be crossed and fingers joined palm to palm. Once the fingers are locked into a large fist, the fist should be rotated up to the COOKIE's chin. This is the safe starting position! The COOKIE should then loudly announce to the group the name of his/her favorite cookie. Players should be thinking about their favorite cookie before they become a COOKIE in the game.

To Play

As soon as the COOKIE MACHINE hears the name of the COOKIE's favorite cookie, they begin chanting in unison the name of the cookie. The COOKIE gets a short running start and dives head first while rotating 180 degrees to land on his/her back onto the COOKIE MACHINE. The COOKIE MACHINE moves the COOKIE by carefully and lightly "bouncing" the COOKIE through the COOKIE MACHINE while continuing the chant. A new COOKIE volunteers to play and the game continues. Players rotate to the front of the line.

87

Game Variations Suggestions

1. Safety: A SPOTTER should be located at the end of the COOKIE MACHINE to assist the COOKIE off the COOKIE MACHINE.
2. More Safety: Have a LEADER monitor height of the COOKIE as it's being passed down the line
3. Play this game on a hill with the "COOKIE" being passed down the hill.

high

energy
level

Quick Description

Sound and Fury- one of the best name games ever with sounds and movement for 8-16 players for elementary to adults. (List of movements**)**

Stand Off- quickly played competitive game used in a mini tournament format for 8-12 players for middle school to adults. (Sticky notes)

Airplane Relay- 5-6 player group relay race with every player being a leader for elementary to adults. (Paper for each team)

Kinzi- unique group jumping game with many variation for 5-40 players for elementary to adults. (Kinzi – a rope with a six inch ring attached)

Group Jump Rope- jumping game with partner teams that keep getting larger for 10-34 players for middle school to adults. (25-35 foot long rope)

Rock, Paper, Scissors Relay- team running competition using the rock/paper/scissors signs and playing one team against another for 10-80 players with teams of 5-8 for middle school to adults. (Five markers per game area)

Stomp and Pop- very fun but competitive elimination game using string and balloons for 10-30 players for middle school to adults. (Balloon and string for each player)

Wink- partner game that requires possibly tackling your partner before they reach an object in the middle of a circle for 11-25 players for middle school to adults. (One object)

Hug Tag- fast moving tag game that provides the players a safety net with other players for 12-30 players for all ages. (No equipment)

Heads and Tails Tag- very interesting continuous motion tag game for 12-30 players for elementary to adults. (No equipment)

Hospital Tag- unique tag game where all players attempt to tag each other until only one player can move for 12-30 players for elementary to adults. (No equipment)

Around and Around- cooperative version of baseball for 12 – 20 players. (Ball, bases and boundary markers)

Octopus- large group high energy tag game where everyone gets caught for 15-40 players for all ages. (No equipment**)**

Blob- action paced group tag game where everyone gets caught for 20-60 players for all ages. (Boundary markers)

Broken Spoke- group "racing and running" game for 21-61 players for all ages. (No equipment)

Wheel and Spokes- team racing competition that pairs up comparable players against each other for a race around the circle of players for 24-64 player and teams of 6-8 for middle school to adults. (Cones, hoop and a bean bag)

sound and fury

To Begin

The players form a circle, standing slightly more than shoulder width apart. The LEADER joins the group and remains a part of the circle with the other players. The LEADER should be familiar with the game and needs to prepare in advance. (See Appendix K - Page 148) from the SOUND AND FURY GAME LIST.

Next

A FURY is a movement or an action. Two examples are: 1) clapping your hands twice or 2) jumping up and down three times. The LEADER provides each player with a FURY. The LEADER should prepare individual FURYS as tabs of paper that will be drawn or selected by each player. Players should not reveal their FURY until the game is played.

Setup

X = Players
O = Leader

Third

The LEADER begins the game by: 1) doing his/her FURY (in this example clap hands twice) and then 2) saying his/her first name (the SOUND). Then, all the players in the circle repeat the STARTER'S FURY and SOUND at the same time. Next, the player to the left of the LEADER performs their FURY and says their name (their SOUND). Again, all of the players around the circle perform that player's FURY and SOUND, and then repeat the STARTER'S FURY and SOUND.

To End

Players continue introducing their FURY and SOUND clockwise around the circle, repeating all the other SOUNDS and FURYS until all players have had a turn. This game should be played quickly, but not too fast. At the end of the game, a player may be called on to go around the circle attempting to name each players SOUND. Another player may be called on to repeat each player's FURY.

Game Variations Suggestions

1. It may be necessary to demonstrate the first two FURYS and SOUNDS and then start over.
2. The LEADER may choose to make the game low energy or high energy

by the FURYS that are selected at the start of the game.

3. Let Players come up with their own actions (FURYS)

Team Building
Competitive Game

stand off

8-36 Players
Middle School to Adult

Equipment:
1 Sticky Note per Player

Play Area:
Indoor or Outdoor

To Begin

STAND OFF is a competitive game between two players at a time. There should be 8-12 players per group. If there is more than one group, players can be grouped according to: 1) size, 2) competitive nature, or 3) gender. Once the grouping has been completed, all of the players write their first name on their own sticky note. Names are then placed randomly one on top or below the others resulting in a LADDER.

Next

The LEADER selects one player for a demonstration. The LEADER and the player face each other. Each player reaches out and places their palms on the shoulders of the other player. Both players start with their feet tight together. Once lined up, each player moves both of their hands to a position in front of their chest with their elbows bent. Both players will have the palms of their hands open and directly across from each other. Each player attempts to "push" the opponent off balance by using their hands only.

Setup

X vs X	Player #1
	Player #2
X vs X	Player #3
	Player #4
X vs X	Player #5
	Player #6
X vs X	Player #7
	Player #8
X vs X	Player #9
	Player #10

Third

Players cannot hit or push shoulders or other body parts. A player wins a round when the opponent loses their balance and moves one or both feet. Two of three rounds are played to determine the winner. After each contest, the winning player will move the names on the LADDER if a successful challenge has occurred. Example: If the third place player beats the first place player, the third place player becomes #1, the former #1 becomes #2 and the #2 player becomes #3. If the original #1 wins, all players stay where they were on the LADDER,

Objective

1. Once play starts, all players may play at the same time by challenging other players on the LADDER.
2. A player may only challenge a player one, two or three positions higher then them on the ladder. (One to two is best).
3. No immediate "challenge backs". Players must challenge and play another player first.
4. Set a time limit for the tournament (10-15 minutes).
5. The LEADER can participate in one of the groups.

91

Game Variations Suggestions

1. At the conclusion, set up a single elimination tournament with all of the players seeded based on results of the LADDER.
2. Monitor safety. Hands on hands only. No grabbing and holding onto hands!
3. See chapter: Tournaments and Motivational Structure for information on Ladders (Page 133).

airplane relay

Equipment: 1 Sheet of Paper per Player
(1) 12'-15' Piece of Rope per Team

Play Area:
Indoor or Outdoor

To Begin

Divide the players into equal teams of five players per team. Each member of each team receives a sheet of paper (8" by 11"). Each player then creates their personal PAPER AIRPLANE. All of the airplanes, except the first leader's airplane (the first player in line) are placed behind the start line. Each team lines up in a single file line behind the start line. The player at the head of the line is the first team PILOT. (Each member of each team will become the team PILOT).

Next

Each single file team has to be connected and stay connected by holding onto a 12-15 foot piece of rope that has a loop in the middle with two ends extending back. The loop goes around the waist of the pilot. On a given signal, the first PILOT in each of the lines (only the first PILOT) "flies" their airplane in the direction of the far goal line. When an airplane is flown, the entire crew while still joined runs together to the location where the airplane has landed. The PILOT picks up the airplane and continues to "fly" it forward until it passes the far goal line.

Setup

X = Players

End Line

Start Line

	XXXXX
	XXXXX
	XXXXX
	XXXXX
30 to 60 Feet	XXXXX

Third

When an airplane passes the end goal line, the entire team can let go of the rope and return quickly to the starting line. The next PILOT takes over with their plane and the rope looped around their waist and the players all holding on to the rope. The first PILOT retreats to the end of the line. The new PILOT continues the same process as the first PILOT. This game continues until every crew member has been a PILOT. The first team to complete the sequence is the winner.
NOTE: Players must use their own airplanes!

Rules

1. PILOTS must fly and retrieve their own airplane. The airplanes may fly forward (best), sideways or backwards (ouch!).
2. All crew members must stay connected by holding tightly on the rope.
3. The player at the front of the line (the PILOT) must race to their own aircraft with the crew connected. The airplane is picked up and flown again from that point.
4. Everyone on each team will have a turn at being the PILOT and to fly their own plane.

Game Variations Suggestions

1. Each player is given a balloon that has to be "flicked" forward. A flick is completed by grasping the open end with one hand and stretching the other end back to- wards the body and then letting go of the balloon.
2. This game could be played with a cloth Frisbee and each player uses the same Frisbee.

Team Building
Collective Score

kinzi

10-30 Players
Upper Elementary to Adult

Equipment:
Kinzi Device

Play Area:
Indoor or Outdoor

To Begin

This activity requires a KINZI (that you can easily make for your play) which is a rope that is 15 - 18 feet long. A weight must be attached to one end of the rope. A standard 6 1/2 inch soft rubber ring or a softball sized whiffle-ball or a foam ball placed in a sock can be used for the weight. Attach the ring or ball securely. The weighted object may come into contact with player's legs or upper body. Keep this in mind when preparing a KINZI.
The ring and rope combination is best.

Next

The players form a circle 20 feet away from the LEADER. The LEADER begins the game in a standing position by swinging the KINZI in a circular pattern just inside the area where the players are standing. The LEADER holds the rope as high as possible and swings the rope slowly at first. The KINZI Device should not be hitting the ground. As the game progresses, the LEADER can speed up the rotation of the KINZI.

Setup

X = Players
O = Leader

● • • • • • • • ○ Kinzi

Third

The players are encouraged to attempt to run to the center of the circle (near the LEADER) and then to run back to safety without getting hit by the KINZI. If a player does get hit, all players return to the starting position and the LEADER begins the swinging motion again.
After awhile, the LEADER will stop play and assume a position on his/her back with the KINZI in hand. The LEADER begins to swing the rope in a low to the ground circular motion around the inside of the circle.

Challenge

Players move into the play area and attempt to "jump rope" over the moving KINZI. If a miss occurs, all players back up and the LEADER begins the swinging motion again. As the players get better and experience success, the LEADER can speed up the rotation of the KINZI.

Players can be encouraged to count out loud the number of successful revolutions before a miss.

93

Game
Variations
Suggestions

1. There are more than 20 different activities that can be played with the KINZI. To view those activities, it is necessary to purchase the KINZI which will be available after further manufacturing.

group jump rope

To Begin

This activity requires a rope that is 25 - 35 feet long and 8 - 12mm thick. An old kernmantle climbing rope is ideal. The LEADER and one volunteer will twirl the rope. Players begin by lining up in a single file line facing the twirlers and the rope.

Next

The twirlers should practice their technique before play begins. The rope must barely touch the ground, the arch should be high and the rotation slow but steady. The rope should be twirled in the opposite direction (away from) of the players.

Setup

X = Players   L = Leader

X

X X X X X X X X X X X X

Rope

L

Rules

1) Play begins with each player (one at a time) approaching the rope and ducking under it and returning to the end of the line.
2) Players approach the rope and attempt two jumps and then exit and return to the line.
3) Players pair up, hold hands, attempt two jumps and then exit and return to the line (3-4 times).
4) Groups of three, hold hands, attempt two jumps and then exit and return to the line (3-4 times).
5) Groups of four (3-4 times).

Rules

6) Groups of eight (2-4 times).

7) Groups of sixteen 2-4 times).

Instead of two revolutions, groups can attempt five or ten. Players should select their partners by the way they have lined up to start the game. The emphasis should be on participation and teamwork, not success. Players should be given multiple opportunities but first must go to the back of the line. The LEADER must attempt to keep action quick paced.

Game Variations Suggestions

1. Players can be encouraged to count out loud the number of successful revolutions before a miss.
2. Play this game in conjunction with BOLA.
3. The LEADER may want to select new twirlers once the game has been played for awhile.

rock, paper, scissors relay

Equipment: Start & Safety Zone Lines 5 Cones/Markers per Game

Play Area: Indoor or Outdoor

To Begin

Players form equal teams of five to eight players. The LEADER arranges the players in two single file lines behind the Start Line and cones. The LEADER demonstrates the ROCK, PAPER and SCISSORS signs and explains that ROCK beats SCISSORS, SCISSORS beats PAPER and PAPER beats ROCK. The LEADER encourages each player to practice the signs. A slow motion walk through demonstration is crucial for this game.

Next

At the Start signal from the LEADER, the first player from each team runs to the outside of the cones past the "Start" and "Point" Lines. The players meet near the far cone. Both players come to a stop and face each other so that team members can watch them "compete". Simultaneously, both players perform a ROCK, PAPER, or SCISSORS. The player that wins continues around the cones in an attempt to cross the "Point Line." In case of a tie, the ROCK, PAPER, SCISSORS game continues until there is a winner.

Setup

X = Team 1   O = Team 2
L = Leader   10

Feet

● ●   X X X X X X

● 30-50 Feet   L

Cone

● ●   O O O O O O

Point Start
Line   Line

Third

The team with the player who does not win the ROCK, PAPER, SCISSORS game, immediately sends its next player out across the "Start" and "Point" Lines and around the cones to confront the other team's player before that player crosses the "Point Line". The players stop and face off with another game of ROCK, PAPER, SCISSORS. The winner moves on, the loser returns to the back of their team line.

Continue

The LEADER should remain in charge of this game to determine when a player has crossed the "Point Line". When a Point is scored, players from both teams immediately begin a new game. Action continues until a set number of points is earned or a time limit is reached. The LEADER should also make sure that players do not Start or cross the Start Line until a Point is scored or until a player on their team has lost. This is a continuous action game and requires players to return to their lines quickly.

95

Game Variations Suggestions

1. With adequate space, this game can be played with multiple teams playing at one time.
2. Set up a mini-tournament. Winners can play winners; losers can play losers, etc.
3. Teams can be responsible to keep track of their own scores once the teams understand how to play the game.

Competitive Game
Tag Game

Equipment: 1 Large Balloon per Player
(1) 30"-36" String per Player

10-34 Players
Middle School to Adult

Play Area:
Indoors

stomp and pop

To Begin

Each player starts the game with a fully inflated 12" balloon and a string. The string should be 30 to 36 inches long. The LEADER should have the materials ready before organizing the players. The play area should be large enough for players to run around but not too large. If possible, the game can be played in a corner with walls on two sides and markers for the boundaries.

Next

Players tie the string to their balloon and then tie the other end of the string to their ankles. There should be 20 - 30 inches of sting extending out to the balloon after it has been tied. The LEADER may have to monitor players to make sure that there is ample string extending. Players can play in gym shoes but not hard soled shoes.

Setup

X = Players with Balloons

Third

Once the string is attached at both ends, players hold onto their balloon so it doesn't break before the game begins. The game begins when the LEADER yells "Go"! Players drop their balloon to the ground and attempt to STOMP and POP other player's balloons while avoiding having their own balloon STOMPED and POPED.

To End

When a player's balloon is POPED, that player must stop play and remain stationary until they count to ten by yelling out loud, "One balloon, two balloons, three balloons", etc. until they reach "ten balloons". They may then resume play in an attempt to break all of the balloons. The last player with an inflated balloon is the winner.

Players may not grab other players or hold onto their own balloons once the game starts.

96

Game

Variations

Suggestions

1. This is a great game to play at the conclusion of BALLOON FRENZY (a good way to break balloons).
2. Safety: Players should be careful to not step on the feet of other players.

3. With enough balloons and a small number of players, a balloon can be tied to each ankle.

Equipment:
1 Frisbee, Bean Bag, and Marker

Play Area:
Carpeted or Grassy

To Begin

There must be an odd number of players to play this game. Each player selects a partner. Players and partners arrange themselves around a circle. The LEADER has no partner and starts the game as the WINKER. A soft surface is recommended.

Next

Partners introduce themselves to each other and to the new partners they meet during the game. One partner then sits cross-legged facing the center of the circle. The other partner kneels behind them. The WINKER also joins the circle in a kneeling position. The WINKER places the OBJECT in front of him/her (instead of a partner).

Setup

X = Players Kneeling
X = Players Sitting
W = WINKER

Third

The action starts when the WINKER gives an obvious WINK to one of the players sitting in the inner circle. This is a sign for that player, the WINKEE, to try to get across the circle to touch the OBJECT. At the same time, the partner of the WINKEE tries to stop them from getting to the OBJECT. The partner does this by holding on to the WINKEE's arms or legs, or by holding the WINKEE down. All of the players not involved in the action being to count, out loud, backwards from "ten" to "zero".

Strategy

If the WINKEE gets to and touches the OBJECT before "zero", he/she and the WINKER become partners, with the WINKEE behind the WINKER. The WINKEE'S old partner becomes the new WINKER. If the WINKEE doesn't get to the OBJECT before "zero", the WINKER must try to find another partner. The game ends when all of the couples have been involved in the WINK action at least once.

97

Game Variations Suggestions

1. The WINKER must exaggerate the wink. The wink should not be confused with a blink.
2. The distance across the circle can be lengthened or shortened depending on the group.

3. Players cannot grab clothing or "fight back" aggressively for safety reasons.

Tag Game
Team Building
Equipment: 3 Foam Balls
4 Cones for Boundaries

hug tag

12-30 Players
Lower Elementary to Adult
Play Area:
Indoor or Outdoor

To Begin

The players scatter throughout the playing area. For a larger number of players, increase the size of the playing area. Smaller boundaries make this game more fun. One player is picked by the LEADER to be the IT. The LEADER can play the game with the other players.

Next

This game is played like a regular game of tag. The IT tries to tag another player with the foam ball (no throwing of the ball). A player who is tagged becomes the new IT. The foam ball is given to the new IT. No immediate tag backs allowed. Any player leaving the play area to avoid being tagged becomes IT automatically.

Setup

X = Players   XX = IT

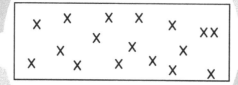

Strategy

If players cannot out run or avoid the IT, they have another way to avoid being tagged. If a Player grabs hold of another player and wraps their arms around them (HUGS them), they both are free from being tagged. Once they leave this position, they can be tagged again by the IT. Players are encouraged to HUG to avoid being tagged!

To Play

A player may only HUG another player for three to five seconds. The IT may not wait for players to stop HUGGING each other. If three or more players HUG each other, the IT may select one of them to be the new IT. If the IT has trouble tagging players, the IT may stop the game and select a new IT.

98

Game Variations Suggestions

1. Once a player is tagged, they have to spin in a complete circle before tag backs.
2. The game can continue with three person HUGS, four persons

HUGS, five person HUGS, etc.

3. The game can be called HOLD TAG with players required to grab hands (no hugging).

Tag Game
Team Building

heads and tails tag

12-30 Players
Upper Elementary to Adult

Equipment: Coin per Player
4 Cones for Boundaries

Play Area:
Indoor or Outdoor

To Begin

Each player starts with a coin which can be provided by the LEADER or coins can be shared. Each player flips the coin, lets it land and becomes a head or a tail. All of the players scatter throughout the playing area. Players should position themselves so other players are not close by and so players have room to run to avoid being tagged. The size of the play area is important. It needs to be large enough for all players to move around freely but small enough so that players can tag each other.

Next

A time limit of two to three minutes should be set. All of the HEADS players begin the game with their left hand on the top of their head. All of the TAIL players begin the game with their left hand on their gluteus (their butt). The LEADER will start the game by yelling, "GO!" The LEADER may want to participate while closely monitoring play.

Setup
X = Players

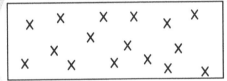

Third

The action involves each team attempting to tag the opposite team players. HEADS attempt to tag TAILS while TAILS attempt to tag HEADS. Only the right hand may be used to tag. Players can be tagged most anywhere on their bodies (not just the head or tail). When a player is tagged, they become transformed. HEADS become TAILS or TAILS become HEADS. Action goes on with the transformed players attempting to tag their opposites.

Objective

The game continues until all of the players are TAILS or HEADS or until the time limit has been reached. Players who leave the play area must kneel immediately upon their return to the play area to wait for the next game to start. If the time limit occurs, the LEADER stops play and counts the number of HEADS and TAILS to determine a winner. Three or four rounds make for a good game.

99

Game Variations Suggestions

1. This is a game of action and honesty. Players must take responsibility for being tagged.
2. After players have been identified as HEADS or TAILS, the LEADER selects one team to play first. In this version, the LEADER times each team (one at a time) to see how long it takes for a team to freeze all of the players on the other team.

hospital tag

Equipment:
4 Cones for Boundaries

Play Area:
Indoor or Outdoor

To Begin

All of the players scatter throughout the playing area. Players should position themselves so other players are not close by and so players have room to run to avoid being tagged. The size of the play area is important. It needs to be large enough for all players to move around freely but small enough so that players can tag each other.

Next

One player is selected to yell "GO!" At the GO signal, every player tries to tag other players. At the same time, each player tries to avoid being tagged by other players. The LEADER may want to participate while closely monitoring play.

Setup
X = Players

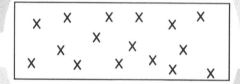

Third

When a player is tagged, they must BANDAGE or cover the part of their body that was tagged. They can do this by using another part of their body, such as their hand, elbows, head, leg, etc. Each time a player gets tagged, they must BANDAGE the new WOUND while continuing to keep the other tags BANDAGED. As long as a player can still move, that player can tag other players!

Rules

Players who cannot cover all WOUNDS must kneel in the playing area. They can no longer tag other players, but instead become obstacles. A player may only tag another player once within five seconds. Players who leave the play area must kneel immediately upon their return to the play area. The last player standing begins the next game by yelling, "GO!"

Game Variations Suggestions

1. This is a game of action and honesty. Players must take responsibility for being tagged.

2. Two players may tag each other at the same time which requires both players to BANDAGE themselves.

3. This is an interesting game to process.

around and around

Equipment: Kickball, Softball, Large
Netball, Bat, Homeplate, 2 Boundaries

Play Area:
Indoor or Outdoor

To Begin

Divide the players into two equal teams of six to ten players per team. One team will be in the field (DEFENSE) and the other team will be at bat (OFFENSE). The DEFENSIVE players scatter around the play area. One player on the DEFENSIVE team is chosen to be the PITCHER, another is the CATCHER. This should rotate every inning. The type of ball selected to play the game depends on player ability, the challenge and the play space. It is important to have an umpire at home plate to determine outs and when runs are scored. The umpire will also keep a running score.

Next

The ball is pitched underhand (or rolled) to the first BATTER from the OFFENSIVE team. The ball is pitched (or rolled) until the BATTER hits it. There are no strike-outs, base-on-balls or fly-outs. The "hit" ball must be in fair territory. Once the ball is "hit", all the DEFENSIVE players form a single file line. The fielder who catches the ball becomes the front of the line. The ball is passed through the first player's legs to the player behind him/her. That player takes the ball and passes it over their head to the player behind them. All players must receive the ball and pass the ball.

Setup

X = Offense   O = Defense

Third

The DEFENSIVE sequence contin-ues (over and under) until the last fielder in the line has the ball. That player must then throw the ball to the CATCHER. When the CATCHER get the ball and tags HOME PLATE, the DEFENSE yells, "OUT!"
Once the ball is "hit", the OFFENSIVE team forms a single file line in foul territory on the third base side of the playing area. The BATTER runs in a counter clockwise circle around that line. The OFFENSIVE team receives one point each time the BATTER circles the team and touches HOME PLATE before the DEFENSE yells, "OUT!"

Continue

Variations to challenge the OF-FENSE can be to have the BATTER run to the back of the line and: 1) weave in and out of each team member or 2) crawl through his/her teams legs to reach home plate.
An inning is over when everyone on both teams has batted once. (If there are six or more players per team, only half of the total number should "bat" each inning.) Teams switch positions to continue the game. Two to six innings make an excellent game. An umpire/scorekeeper is advised.

Game Variations Suggestions

1. Place bases on the field or floor (1st, 2nd, 3rd and home). The DE-FENSE must pass the ball "over and under" until there are four players left. Those players must catch the ball while standing on each of the bases with home plate being the last base. Rotate the players on the bases.

Competitive Game
Tag Game

Equipment:
4 Cones for Boundaries

octopus

15-40 Players
Lower Elementary to Adult

Play Area:
Indoor or Outdoor

To Begin

One player is selected to be the OCTO-PUS. The OCTOPUS stands near middle of the play area facing the other players. All of the other players line up behind one of the goals. They are the FISH. The area in-between the goals is the OCEAN.

Next

The OCTOPUS calls out loudly, "FISH, FISH, COME SWIM IN MY OCEAN!" At this command, all of the FISH try to get to the other goal line without being tagged by the OCTOPUS. The OCTOPUS attempts to tag as many FISH as possible. The OCTOPUS may roam over the entire OCEAN (the play area).

Setup

X= FISH

X X X X X X X X X X X X X X X

Goal Line	
O	30-60 Feet
Goal Line	

30-100 Feet

O= OCTOPUS

Third

When a FISH is tagged, they must remain in the place they were tagged until all the other FISH have crossed the OCEAN. They then become TENTACLES of the OCTOPUS. The TENTACLES kneel down and extend their arms while remaining in the spot where they were tagged. The TENTACLES try to tag FISH as they pass by after the OCTOPUS calls out. "FISH, FISH, COME SWIM IN MY OCEAN!"

To End

The game continues until all of the FISH have been caught (tagged). FISH must not leave the boundaries of the OCEAN or they will be considered CAUGHT. If they leave the play area, they must kneel down closest to where they went out of bounds. Once all of the FISH have been tagged, the game ends. Another game is started with the last FISH to be tagged becoming the new OCTOPUS!

102

1. With a large play space, it may be necessary to start the game with two OCTOPUSES.
2. Safety can be a concern in this game with players running and

dodging the OCTOPUS.
3. It is important to start the game with an OCTOPUS who can catch FISH. The OCPOTUS gets tired as the game progresses

blob

To Begin

Use boundary markers to identify the rectangular play area. The size of the playing field is important in this game. It may require adjustment. All of the players stand behind the same goal line at the start. Make sure there is enough room behind each goal line for players to run past the goal line and to stop safely. The game starts with two one person BLOBS. Two players are selected to be the BLOBS. The BLOBS will stand anywhere in the play area facing the players on the goal line.

Next

One of the BLOBS is responsible for starting the game. The BLOB yells, "GO!" and all of the players run through the play area and across the opposite goal line. The BLOBS attempts to tag as many players as possible before they cross the goal line. Tagging is done with the hands only. NOTE: The BLOBS may tag more than one player. Players that step out of the playing area while attempting to avoid a BLOB become part of a BLOB during the next round.

Setup

X = Players   O = BLOB

X X X X X X X X X X X X X X

Goal Line

O

30-60 Feet

Goal Line
30-100 Feet

Third

As soon as the BLOB tags a player, the player joins hands with one end of the BLOB and that player becomes part of the BLOB. The "new" BLOB sets out, hand-in-hand, attempting to tag more players. Once all of the players have crossed the opposite goal line, the BLOB can split into two or more smaller BLOBS. Each BLOB requires two or more players (No single player BLOBS after the first round). Remember, the BLOB can only split after all of the players have crossed one of the goal lines.

Strategy

Once all of the Players have crossed the opposite goal line and the BLOB has split and scattered throughout the play area, the original BLOB again yells, "GO!" and players must run back to the other goal line. More and more players will become part of a BLOB. Only the outside hands of the BLOB can tag players. The game is over when the last player is tagged by the BLOB. The last two players tagged can become the new BLOBS for the next game.

103

Team Building
Tag Game
Equipment:
None

21-61 Players
Lower Elementary to Adult
Play Area:
Indoor or Outdoor

broken spoke

To Begin

Divide all the players into groups (SPOKES) of four to ten per spoke. There should be at least four SPOKES, but not more than six. The LEADER stands at the center of the play area and calls for all the players born in January through March to gather in a single file line facing the LEADER. The LEADER then turns to the right and calls for all the players born in April through June to line up facing the center. This continues until all the spokes are filled. For six spokes, use only two months per spoke.

Next

It may be necessary to make adjustments in Spoke size. After the players are organized into equal sized SPOKES, all players all kneel or sit down. Each SPOKE is a separate team. The game begins with the players kneeling (or sitting) in single file lines, like the SPOKES of a wheel, each facing the center or HUB of the wheel. The LEADER is the first IT. The LEADER starts at the back of all the SPOKES.

Setup

X = Players O = IT

Third

The IT walks around the outside of the circle and taps the last player in each SPOKE. The IT yells one of three commands as they tap each player: "STAY", "FOLLOW ME" or "RUN AWAY". When the IT says "STAY", all players in the SPOKE remain in place. If the IT says "FOLLOW ME", all players in the SPOKE chase the IT around the circle and back to their single file SPOKE. If the IT says "RUN AWAY" all players in that SPOKE run around the circle in the opposite direction of the IT and return back to their SPOKE.

Strategy

Once the IT gives a command, the IT also races around the other kneeling (or sitting) SPOKES of the circle and back to the BROKEN SPOKE. The last player to return and kneel (or sit) in the single file BROKEN SPOKE is the new IT. It is important that players listen to the IT and that the IT yells loudly. Players must run around the circle and be careful not to collide with other runners or stationary players. There is NO jumping across any of the SPOKES. Every SPOKE should get a chance to play.

104

Game

Variations

Suggestions

1. Movement variations have the best results. Have the players skip, walk backward, hop, etc.
2. Set cones a distance (10 - 30 feet) behind all of the SPOKES so that the

players will have to run a longer distance (more aerobic).

3. Allow the IT to select more than one SPOKE at a time.

Relay Game
Competitive Game

Equipment:
6 Cones, Hula Hoops, Bean Bags

24-64 Players
Middle School to Adult

Play Area:
Indoor or Outdoor

wheel and spokes

To Begin

Six to eight players are required for each team. The game is played with four to six teams. Let's assume there forty-two players which will play the game with six teams of seven players each. The LEADER tells all of the players to find seven players with about the same athletic ability as themselves. The LEADER assigns a number from one to seven for each group. Six groups will be identified. The play area is set up (see organizational pattern). The LEADER stands in the center of the hula hoop.

Next

The LEADER calls for all of the "ones" to gather around the outside of the hula hoop. The LEADER arranges the six players equi-distant apart facing the center. The LEADER calls for all of the "twos" to stand behind one of the "ones". The LEADER calls for all of the "threes" to stand in one of the SPOKES behind a "one" and a "two". This continues until all players are lined up in a seven player SPOKE facing the middle. All of the players must remember their original number!

Setup

X= Players C= Cone
L= Leader

O= Hula Hoop

Third

The cones are placed behind and midway between all of the SPOKES. The LEADER places a bean bag (or similar object) in the center of the hula hoop. The LEADER moves to a position between two of the SPOKES. The LEADER will remind all players to remember their original numbers. When players are ready, the LEADER will loudly call out one of the numbers.

To Play

All of the players with that number quickly step to their right and run to the back of their line and continue to run around the entire WHEEL clockwise making sure to run outside of the cones. When a player gets back to their SPOKE, they must crawl through the legs of all of their teammates and attempt to grab the bean bag before players from other teams grab the bean bag. The player who grabs the bean bag earns one point for their team. The game ends when each player (number) has had a turn (or two).

105

Game Variations Suggestions

1. Change the movement when players move around the circle to skipping, hopping, and walking backward, etc.

2. Move the cones back further to create a longer run.

3. Play on a mat or grassy surface.

very high energy level

Quick Description

Triangle Tag- wild attempt by a player to grab an object from three other players for 4-40 players with groups of four for middle school to adults. (Bandana per group)

Go Tag- continuous motion tag game with strategy and team work for 8-12 players for middle school to adults. (No equipment)

World's Fastest Tag Game- the world's fastest tag game for 10-30 players for all ages. (Boundary markers)

Catch the Dragons Tail- group challenge and competitive game for teams of 5-8 players for middle school to adults. (1 bandana for each team)

Freeze Tag- fast action group tag game that allows players to save each other for 12-30 players for all ages. (Boundary markers)

Elbow Tag- quick paced tag game for 12-30 players for all ages. (No equipment)

Pairs and Pairs Squared- fast moving tag game within a tag game with partners for 12-40 players. (Boundary markers)

Side by Side Tag- quick paced tag game with most players laying on the ground for 12-30 players for all ages. (No equipment)

British Bulldog- very physical "catch the opponent" game for 12-30 players for middle school to adults. (Boundary markers)

Dho, Dho, Dho!- physical and strategic tag game for 12-30 players for high school to adults. (Boundary markers)

Taffy Pull- very physical team versus team challenge to pull each team away from team members for 16-30 players for high school to adult. (Tape for boundary)

Tag Game
Competitive Game
Equipment:
1 Bandanna per Group

triangle tag

4-40 Players
Middle School to Adult
Play Area:
Indoor or Outdoor

To Begin

Players form into groups of fours. Groups scatter throughout the play area making sure there is sufficient space between groups to allow movement for the game to be played. One of the players in each groups is chosen to be the IT for that group. NOTE: The game can be started and played with multiple groups.

Next

A second player from each group is chosen to be the TARGET. The TARGET places a bandanna or sock under their belt or in their back pocket so that it dangles behind them. Then, the TARGET and the other two players, not the IT, form a TRIANGLE by facing each other and grasping each others forearms with their hands.

Setup
X = Players IT = IT

Third

The TRIANGLE gets into position with the IT on the outside and away from the TARGET. When the players are ready, the IT says, "GO!" and tries to grab the object dangling behind the TARGET. Without breaking their grip, the TRIANGLE works together to keep the IT from getting the TARGET. The TRIANGLE may only move left or right.

To End

Play continues for 60 to 90 seconds or until the IT gets the TARGET's object (or is too tired to keep playing). The IT may make limited contact with the TRIANGLE to confuse or trick them, but the IT may not reach across the TRIANGLE to break the player's grips. Another player in the circle volunteers to be the new IT. Play continues until all players have had a chance to be the IT and the TARGET.

108

Game Variations Suggestions

1. Each member of the TRIANGLE may only move by hopping on one foot.
2. One or two players in the triangle can be blindfolded.

3. Play the game with a rectangle by adding an additional player to game (5 per group). Very difficult.

Tag Game
Competitive Game
Equipment:
None

go tag

8-12 Players
Middle School to Adult
Play Area:
Indoor or Outdoor

To Begin

The LEADER arranges all of the players shoulder to shoulder while standing in a straight line facing one direction. Once the LEADER explains the rules, players alternate facing forward and backward while remaining in a straight line. Players can arrange their feet one in front of the other in order to run quickly. A player at one end of the line is the first IT and a player at the other end is the RUNNER. The LEADER may want to join in the game as a player.

Next

The LEADER may choose to play this game. When players are ready, the LEADER yells, "GO!" At the GO signal, every player tries to tag other players. At the same time, each player tries to avoid being tagged by other players.

Setup

X= Players
O= IT
R= Runner

O

X X X X X X X X X

R

Third

The IT works with the other players to tag the RUNNER. As the IT is chasing the RUNNER around the line, the IT can tap any player on the back who is facing the other direction and yell "GO!". (The IT cannot tap players that are facing them). The player tapped becomes the new IT and must start the chase in the direction they are facing. The old IT quickly replaces the new IT's position in the line. Note: Only the IT can tap another player. The RUNNER must continue until tagged.

Strategy

Walk when you first play this game and practice the GO-TAG manuever. The key to this game is to change ITS often. Everyone should have an oportunity to be the IT and the RUNNER. It may be necessary to stop the game to allow the outside players in the line an opportunity to switch to a middle position after the game has been played for awhile. NOTE: The IT will always be able to tag the RUNNER if multiple ITS are selected throughout the game.

109

Game Variations Suggestions

1. More than one GO TAG game can be played at one time if there are more than 12 players.
2. Once a RUNNER is tagged by the IT, the RUNNER must spin in a circle before tagging the new RUNNER.
3. Change movement options: have the players walk fast, skip, hop, move in slow motion, etc.

worlds fastest tag game

To Begin

All of the players scatter throughout the playing area. Players should position themselves so other players are not close by, and so players have room to run and not be tagged immediately.

Next

All of the players scatter throughout the playing area. Players should position themselves so other players are not close by, and so players have room to run and not be tagged immediately.

Setup
X = Players

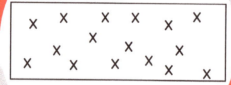

Third

When a player is tagged, they can no longer tag other players. A tagged player must immediately kneel down, which lets other players know they have been tagged. Kneeling players now become obstacles for other players to dodge around. Players should be careful not to run into any kneeling players. Kneeling players may not tag other players.

Rules

Players who have not been tagged continue to try tagging other players. If two players tag each other at the same time, they both must kneel. Players who leave the playing area must kneel immediately upon their return to the play area. The game ends when one player is left standing. That player starts the next game by yelling, "GO!"

Game Variations Suggestions

1. The size of the play space can determine how quickly the game is completed. Keep the space small enough so that the game ends in one to three minutes.

2. Play the game with partners who run with arms locked at the elbow. Only one partner needs to be touched before both players kneel.

Tag Game
Competitive Game
Equipment:
1 Bandana per Group

10-40 Players
Middle School to Adult
Play Area:
Indoor or Outdoor

catch the dragons tail

To Begin

Players are divided into (DRAGONS) of five to eight players per DRAGON. If there is more than one DRAGON, each DRAGON should have an equal number of players. The DRAGONS line up in a straight line away from the other DRAGONS.

Next

The player at the front end of the DRAGON becomes the HEAD of the DRAGON, while the player at the end of the line becomes the DRAGON'S TAIL END. The TAIL END places or tucks a sock or towel (the TAIL) into their belt or the waistband of their pants near the small of his/her back. Each player in the DRAGON, except the HEAD, places both of their arms around the waist of the player in front of them. Player's fingers can be joined but not interlocked.

Setup
X = Players

Head → X X X X X X X ←
↓ X X X X X X X ↙ Tail

Third

When the LEADER yells, "GO!", the HEAD of the DRAGON tries to grab the TAIL hanging from the DRAGON'S TAIL END. The TAIL END tries to avoid having the TAIL grabbed. The players in between hold on and move with the HEAD and the TAIL END. When the TAIL is grabbed by the HEAD, or if the line breaks (hands come apart), the HEAD of the DRAGON moves to the end of the line and becomes the new TAIL END and all of the other players move forward one position in the DRAGON line.

Continue

Play continues until all players have had one turn at all of the positions in the DRAGON. If there is more than one DRAGON, (after playing the first version), have each DRAGON try to grab the TAIL hanging from the TAIL END of another DRAGON. Once a DRAGON'S TAIL is grabbed or if the DRAGON breaks apart, that DRAGON is dead and must stand in place as an obstacle for other DRAGONS.

Game Variations Suggestions

1. Start this game off by having the DRAGON walk fast (no running).
2. Players that are part of the DRAGON may need to adjust how they secure themselves to the player in front of them.
3. Safety: Players must be wearing tennis shoes. No bare feet, stocking feet or hard soled shoes!

Tag Game
Collective Score
Equipment: 3-6 Colored Bandanas
4 Cones for Boundaries

freeze tag

12-30 Players
Lower Elementary to Adult
Play Area:
Indoor or Outdoor

To Begin

The players scatter throughout the playing area. The size of the play area is very important. For a larger number of players, increase the size of the playing area. One IT is picked for every six players. The ITS wear the bandanas or the pinnies so they can be easily recognized by the players. (They could also carry a foam ball or other object to identify them as being the ITS).

Next

When the players are ready to play, one of the ITS yells, "GO!" The ITS try to tag the players. When a player is tagged, they must FREEZE in their tagged position. It is acceptable for a tagged player to take one or two more steps so they can FREEZE with their legs spread wide apart in the play area. Players that leave the play area to avoid being tagged must return to the play area and are immediately FROZEN.

Setup

X = Players XX = IT

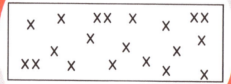

Third

Players not tagged continue to avoid the ITS while trying to THAW any FROZEN players. This is done by crawling through a FROZEN player's legs. After a player THAWS a FROZEN player, both are allowed to continue the game. If a player gets tagged while attempting to THAW a FROZEN player, that player may stand up and assume a position with their legs spread wide apart so that they have the opportunity to be THAWED by the players not yet FROZEN.

Objective

There are two endings for this game:

1. When all of the players are FROZEN, the game is over. The ITS can choose new ITS to start another game.

2. If the ITS cannot FREEZE the players in three to four minutes, the game needs to be stopped. New ITS should be picked and an extra IT or two may be added to the game.

Game

Variations

Suggestions

1. Movement patterns may be changed, i.e., skipping, walking fast, walking backward, giant steps, marching, etc.

2. Safety: Players need to make sure that two players do NOT attempt to crawl under a FROZEN players legs at the same time in an effort to THAW them!

elbow tag

Equipment:
None

Play Area:
Indoor or Outdoor

To Begin

There should be an even number of players for this game to be played. All of the players choose a partner. If there are an odd number of players, one partner group will have three players. Partners stand next to each other facing the same direction with both of their hands on their hips forming a triangle. Partners lock their inside elbows together forming a joined triangle.

Next

All of the teams of partners scatter around the play area making sure they are not too close to any of the other groups but also not too far away. There must be room to easily run between pairs of players. Teams of partners can face in any direction. One team of partners is selected from all of the partner groups to begin the game. One partner will start the game as the RUNNER and the other partner will start the game as the IT.

Setup

X = Players O = Runner
OO = IT

XX   XX   O

XX

XX

XX   XX

XX   XX

OO

Third

The RUNNER attempts to avoid being tagged by the IT. If the RUNNER is tagged, they become the new IT and can immediately tag back. The RUNNER can avoid being tagged by dodging the IT or by locking elbows with any other player from one of the partner groups.

To End

When the RUNNER locks their elbows with the outside elbow of another player, that player's partner becomes the new RUNNER and must run away from the IT.

Start this game at a slow pace. Encourage the RUNNER to lock elbows with other players so everyone can play. If the IT is having trouble tagging the RUNNER, the IT can choose another player to be the IT at any time.

113

Game Variations Suggestions

1. Tag Back Rule: Once a player is tagged, they must spin in a circle before chasing the player who tagged them (or both players can spin).

2. Change the movement pattern. Have players walk, skip, walk backward, etc.

Tag Game
Team Building

pairs & pairs squared

12-40 Players
Upper Elementary to Adult

Equipment:
4 Cones for Boundaries

Play Area:
Indoor or Outdoor

To Begin

This is a tag game. Each player selects a partner of equal athletic ability. An even number of players is needed. The LEADER can play if necessary. The boundaries need to be carefully considered, small enough to contain all of the players and large enough for everyone to move around without bumping into each other. Too large an area is also not ideal. Once partners are determined, one partner agrees to be the IT and the other partner becomes the RUNNER.

Next

Every player has a partner to start the game. The IT must tag the RUNNER. Players may only tag their own partners. When a RUNNER is tagged, they spin in a circle before a tag back is allowed. Players must walk (or walk fast). NO Running! Players must stay within the boundaries. If the RUNNER goes out of the boundaries, they become the new IT. The LEADER monitors play. Players will become tired very quickly.

Setup

A-Run	B-IT	C-IT	F-Run
G-IT	F-IT		
D-Run			A-IT
		E-Run	D-IT
E-IT	C-Run		
G-Run			B-Run

A-Run - Runner "A"
A-IT - IT "A"
B-Run - Runner "B"
B-IT - IT "B"

Third

Allow players to briefly rest after the PAIRS game. The LEADER has each partner group select another pair as new partners (PAIRS SQUARED). If there are an odd number of partners, one group can play with three person groups. Once partner groups are determined, one partner group agrees to be the IT and the other partner group becomes the RUNNERS.

Objective

Rules are similar to the PAIRS game. Partner groups must lock elbows as they move through the play area. Only one IT has to make a tag. Only one partner in a group needs to be tagged. When a RUNNER group is tagged, they spin in a circle before a tag back is allowed. Partner groups CANNOT squeeze between other partner groups who are joined. The LEADER monitors play. Players will become tired very quickly.

114

Game Variations Suggestions

1. Use different modes of movement (skipping, walking backward, giant steps, etc.)
2. Provide each partner group with a ball. The IT must tag the RUNNER

with the ball.
3. The PAIRS SQUARED version of the game may slow down the speed of players who have difficulty with the NO Running rule.

side by side tag

To Begin

There should be an even number of players for this game to be played. All of the players choose a partner. If there are an odd number of players, one partner group will have three players. Partners lie on their stomachs next to each other scattered at random around the play space. It is important to arrange partner groups so that they are not all facing the same direction or in an orderly formation.

Next

After the teams have been scattered around the play area, the LEADER makes sure they are not too close to any of the other groups but also not too far away. There must be room to easily run between pairs of players. One team of partners is then selected to start the game. One player from that team will start the game as the RUNNER and the other player will start the game as the IT.

Setup

X = Players O = Runner
OO = IT

XX   XX   O

XX

XX   XX

XX   XX   OO

Third

The RUNNER attempts to avoid being tagged by the IT. If the RUNNER is tagged, they become the new IT and can immediately tag back. The RUNNER can avoid being tagged by dodging the IT or by lying down next to any of the teams of partners scattered throughout the play area. When lying down, the RUNNER must be facing in the same direction as the partner team on the ground.

Rules

When the RUNNER lies down next to a player, that player's partner becomes the new RUNNER and must get up and run away from the IT.

Start this game at a slow pace. Encourage the RUNNER to switch with other players so everyone can play. If the IT is having trouble tagging the RUNNER, choose another player to be the IT.

115

Game Variations Suggestions

1. Tag Back Rule: Once a player is tagged, they must spin in a circle before chasing the player who tagged them (or both players can spin).

2. Change the movement pattern. Have players walk, skip, walk backward, etc.

Team Building
Competitive Game
Equipment:
4 Cones for Boundaries

12-30 Players
Middle School to Adult
Play Area:
Indoor or Outdoor

british bulldog

To Begin

When setting up the play area, keep the distance between goal lines to no more than 15 feet and the width of the goal lines between 30 and 75 feet (the more players, the wider the area). The LEADER should select one IT for every three to four players. (The ITS should be the biggest and the strongest players). Please remember to stress safety while playing this game! A matted or grass playing area is advised. A LEADER must monitor this game closely!

Next

The ITS take a position in the middle of the play area. All of the players line up behind the same goal line and face the ITS (the British Bulldogs). One of the ITS slowly counts, "1-2-3" and then all of the ITS yell, "BRITISH BULLDOG!" At this command, all of the players try to run (or walk) across the play area over to the other side of the goal line.

Setup

O= BRITISH BULLDOGS

X X X X X X X X X X X X X X

Goal Line

O O O O O

15 Feet

Goal Line

30-75 Feet

X= Players

Third

When the players enter the play area, the ITS attempt to catch the players before they reach the other goal line. To be caught, a player must be picked up off the ground by one or more ITS while the ITS yell, "BRITISH BULLDOG 1-2-3!" The player's body must be kept off the ground during the entire chant. If any part of the player's body touches the ground or crosses the opposite goal line, the Player has not been caught by the ITS and is still safe.

Strategy

Once a player is caught, they join the team of ITS during the next round and try to catch other players. The game continues with players running from one goal line to the other until all of the players are caught.

Players cannot be tackled to the ground by the ITS. Players cannot kick or hit to avoid being caught. If a player does not like physical contact, let them watch from the out-of-bounds or allow them to be ITS. NOTE: This can be a very combative and aggressive game.

116

Game Variations Suggestions

1. Consider single gender options, boys against boys and girls against girls.

2. Special gear: Use this game as a special drill during football practice.

3. Give players an option to play or not play.

4. Be aware of "touching" issues.

Team Building
Competitive Game
Equipment:
8 Cones for Boundaries

dho, dho, dho!

12-30 Players
High School to Adult
Play Area:
Padded or Grassy

To Begin

Divide the players into two equal teams. Each team will start by standing in a zone opposite each other but not in the NEUTRAL ZONE. The game LEADER demonstrates the game, monitors play and makes DHO, DHO, DHO decisions as play progresses. Note: The LEADER must be familiar with the game and the game rules.

Next

Each team picks a player from their team to be the IT. Decide which team will go first. The IT is the only player who can cross the NEUTRAL ZONE to enter the opposite teams play area. The IT cannot be touched by the other team until the IT touches someone first. Never allow more than one IT to DHO, DHO, DHO at a time!

A new IT will be chosen from each team during the game as play rotates from one side to the other until each player has had at least one turn to be the IT.

Setup

10 Feet

Neutral Zone

X X X X

X X X

X X X

XX X

30 Feet

25 Feet   25 Feet

X = Team A
O = Team B

Third

The IT chosen to go first takes a deep breath before crossing the NEUTRAL ZONE. The IT must then cross the NEUTRAL ZONE and run into the other team's play area. The IT may attempt to tag a player or players from the other team and return safely to their team area. The IT must repeat the chant, "DHO, DHO, DHO!" loudly and continuously, and in only one breath. Note: The IT does not have to tag players from the other team but may want to enter the other teams play space and then return safely to their own team area.

To Play

When and if a player from the opposite team is touched, any member from that team can catch and hold the IT until he/she runs out of breath (No Tackling). The IT then joins their team. If the IT makes it back across the NEUTRAL ZONE without running out of breath, all those tagged or touched by the IT join the IT's team. Players that enter the NEUTRAL ZONE or go out of the boundary lines also become members of the IT's team. The teams alternate until everyone is on the same team or until everyone has had one turn to be IT.

117

Game Variations Suggestions

1. Start this game with a slow motion demonstration. The first couple of rounds may want to be played while walking rather than running mode.

2. The LEADER needs to take charge and keep this game safe!
3. Players may choose to not become assertive or active. This should be demonstrated.

Team Building
Competitive Game
Equipment:
Masking Tape or Cones

16-30 Players
High School to Adult
Play Area:
Indoor or Outdoor

taffy pull

To Begin

This is a high energy game with much physical touching. Divide the players into two equal teams. A good method to accomplish this is to have all of the players find a partner about the same size as themselves. Line up the players across from each other so they are facing their partners. One team is chosen to be the TAFFY, the other team will be the TAFFY PULLERS. The TAFFY all enter the inner 10 foot circle. The circle can be established using masking tape or the inner circle of a wrestling mat. Another circle should be established five or more feet outside the inner circle.

Next

The TAFFY PULLERS all line up around the outside of the outer circle. A LEADER should monitor the game at all times and be ready to stop play if necessary. The TAFFY arrange themselves into a tight, inter-locked formation. They do this by lying down, sitting or standing and grabbing other team member's hands, legs, etc. When the TAFFY is "stuck together" as best as possible, play begins.

Setup

X = Players Outside Circle
O = Players Inside Circle

5 ft | 10 ft

Third

When the TAFFY is ready, the LEADER yells, "START!" The TAFFY PULLERS move in to the circle and attempt to pull the TAFFY apart and out of both circles. Once a TAFFY is pulled completely out of both circles, they cannot re-enter. TAFFY PULLERS should only grab TAFFY by hands, arms or legs. They must not grab the head, neck, or any clothing. TAFFY must not "fight back" with the TAFFY PULLERS by swinging arms or kicking legs.

Safety

If at anytime a player or the LEADER yells, "STOP PLAY!" all players must stop instantly! TAFFY PULLERS can work together to pull TAFFY apart, but all players must be careful so no one gets hurt. TAFFY and TAFFY PULLERS switch roles after all TAFFY have been pulled apart and out of both circles.

The LEADER may want to give players the option of not being a TAFFY by allowing them to help with timing and safety.

Game Variations Suggestions

1. The LEADER must monitor the game for safety.
2. The LEADER can time each group to determine how quickly each team can complete the goal

3. This is a great game for a wrestling team warm up or for football players in pads.

GAME MATRIX – AN EXPLANATION

What is the game matrix? It is a consistent attempt to present a framework or model from which all of the games in this book can be examined, learned and taught. There are many "game" books that have been written. Very seldom has there been a consistent framework of components that all games have in common. The game matrix seeks to respond to the questions, "What are common components in all games?" and "What if all games were prepared while taking into consideration common components?" The answer and the result of those questions can be observed in all of the 100 games in the book. All of the "very best group" games include eight common components. Each component will be identified and explained briefly. See the "King Frog" example to the right:

Key Component	Explanation	Example
NAME	The name of the game should be helpful and fun. It may tell something about what happens when the game is played. There are many games that have different names but that are played the same way. The only thing different may be the name.	King Frog
ENERGY LEVEL	Four energy levels are listed. 1) Low energy games involve less movement. 2) Medium energy games can be played by most anyone but take more effort and skill. 3) High energy games need players who give big efforts (running, dodging, etc.) and skill (catching, throwing, etc.). 4) Very high energy games need players who move a lot who have special skills such as lifting or tackling players.	Low Energy
NUMBER OF PLAYERS	There are three key numbers: 1) minimum or the least amount of players for a game to be played; 2) maximum or the most players for a game to be played, and 3) ideal which may be a number between the minimum and maximum.	Minimum 5 Maximum 14 Ideal 7–12
EQUIPMENT	The basic gear or needed to play the game. In some cases it is okay to replace or add to the basic gear.	None
PLAY AREA	The space for safely and successfully playing the game based on type of activity, the kind of game or the safety of the players.	Any indoor or outdoor area
ORGANIZATIONAL PATTERN	A diagram or explanation of how the players and the leader will "line-up" to start the game.	
GAME VARIATIONS AND CHANGES	Each change creates a different game. Changes are made to increase or decrease IT Power or to make the game safer and more fun.	A "Fishbowl" approach for larger groups
GAME DESCRIPTION	The description for each game is about how to play the game. It includes rules, strategy, and other information that players need to know to play the game.	Key information: How do you play the game?

KEY TERMINOLOGY – DEFINITIONS AND EXAMPLES

Competitive Games- Competitive games present a situation or challenge where a skill-perceived task (the activity or the game) is determined by performing better than one's opponent. The primary goal and the usual result of a competition is one team or individual wins and the other team, teams or individual/s lose. Emphasis is placed on the outcome of the game or activity. Many, if not most, of the games that are played today are competitive games where elimination of other individuals or teams based on skill (and luck), is accepted and is the standard. There is a place for these type of games but if play is important and fun, it doesn't always serve the majority of participants well by placing such a high regard for rewarding the best at the expense of those who may need it the most. Some of the games in this book are competitive. A short chapter is devoted to explain competitive methods to enhance the game experience for participants in these types of contests. See "Tournaments and Motivational Structure" page 125.

Cooperative Games- Cooperative games present a situation or challenge where success on a skill-perceived task (the activity or the game) is determined by a joint or cooperative effort with other participants toward achieving some goal. The primary goal should be of common interest to the group. The reward achieved during the process of the game should be one that could not be realized by working alone or against one another. Emphasis is placed on the game process, and the result of the activity is usually predetermined. The majority of the games in this book fall into the "cooperative" category. Games can be fun for everyone, all ages and all skill levels.

Cooperative Competition- Cooperative competition is a situation or challenge where a skill-perceived task (the activity or the game) is determined by teammates working together cooperatively to achieve a pre-conceived goal. Although the result of a cooperative competition is usually a winner and a loser (or a winner and losers), the outcome is never as important as the process. This type of competition is more individualized, with the players always more important than the goal. Most of the competitive games in this book are played with this emphasis.

Game Flow- Game Flow is a principle of the game change based on Csikxzentmihalyi's concept of the "flow experience". According to this theory, "fun" or the "play experience" lies somewhere between boredom and anxiety. Game flow can be controlled by utilizing "IT Power" and proper game leadership techniques. Stopping a game at its peak is a method to enhance game flow.

Collective Score- Collective score is a game scoring technique in which groups or individuals work together to score as high a total as possible. A collective score usually records the number of attempts in a sequence where no misses or errors are made. Examples include playing table tennis (counting how many hits are made in a row without a miss) or playing softball (counting the number of balls caught by a team before a miss). As the "score" gets higher, the intensity and excitement builds until a miss occurs.

GROUP GAMES UNIT – KEY PARTS OF ALL GAMES– Assignment #3

Game Matrix- The game matrix is a consistent attempt to present a framework or model from which all of the games in this book can be examined, learned and taught. By categorizing the many components of a game, one is able to provide a model. This model allows activity leaders to design, change or adapt the structure of any game to enhance a specific psycho-motor, social or emotional outcome. See Game Matrix – An Explanation (Page 113) for a more thorough explanation.

Game Jigsawing- Jigsawing is a cooperative method of leading a game which involves dividing the description of the game into four sequential sections. Each section of the Jigsaw contains information relevant to the game being properly played. Sections can include: Before Beginning, To Play, Strategy, Rules, How to End, etc. These partial explanations of the game are distributed to individuals in the cooperative leading groups. The group members then get together and share their knowledge with other group members until the game is understood. Groups then practice the game. Finally, the group presents and leads the game to the other members of the class or to other participants. The amount and type of information provided in the Jigsaw is dependent upon the specific game and the type of learning. See Effective Cooperative (Group) Instruction - Individual Accountability (Page 124).

Creative Game Matrix- The matrix is a creative game teaching and playing technique based on the notion of forcing associations among and between game related elements. Six categories are identified and given specific information. A random selection of an element in each category results in a potential creative game experience. Groups of players undertake the challenge of cooperatively creating a game from the random information. The matrix presented to you offers the possibility of 2,985,984 different combinations of games. Each of the six categories contains twelve elements. To use the matrix, a number can be assigned to each of the twelve elements per category. An individual or a cooperative group selects a number (from one to twelve) for each of the categories. A number is selected six times (once for each category). These elements then become the specific information for a game to be created. See Creative Game and Play Matrix (Page 130) and (Page 139) for a larger Play Matrix to plan from.

Stop Play Rule- Any player or leader, at any time may yell "STOP PLAY" and all other players will immediately stop action. In all game and play activities, the safety of the player is most important. Therefore, it is necessary to create a verbal signal that informs all other players that an individual's safety is at stake or that an injury may have occurred. Any player or leader may yell "STOP PLAY" when they feel they are in a situation where an injury has or may occur or that a dangerous situation exists. When players hear the STOP PLAY command, they will stop their activity immediately.

PLAY STATEMENTS AND QUOTES

The following statements and quotes were accumulated through the years and used for discussion and thought. They are not the author's words or necessarily the author's opinion. They are not placed in a particular order. (The author's apology for not directly citing the source of these statements.) They are valuable, however, and useful in the context of this book.

1. Play- A free time activity standing quite consciously outside "ordinary" life as being not serious but at the same time absorbing the player intensely and utterly.

2. Play occurs within certain limits of space, time and meaning- it's done by all healthy children.

3. Play must be chosen voluntarily (self initiated) because it is pleasing and fun, intrinsically gratifying and has no goal other than itself (conceived as the opposite of work).

4. A person at play delights in seeking out challenges and overcoming them.

5. An activity might be said to approximate play in inverse proportion to the extent to which it is rule bound.

6. Play is the work of children and is generally carried on by children (and some adults)

7. Most definitions of play do seem to exclude competitive activities.

8. Play is to be played exactly because it isn't serious; it frees us from seriousness.

9. Clearly competition and play tug in two different directions- if you are trying to win; you are not engaged in true play.

10. Play is not concerned with quantifying because there is no performance to be quantified.

11. The majority of children to drop out of organized play or sport indicated that they dropped out because "they never let me play."

12. A system which makes "being good" a prerequisite to playing would not appear to be recreational or in the best interest for the majority of children.

13. During play, any activity, no matter how trivial, can become the most important event of life at the moment.

14. In North America it is not uncommon to lose 80% - 90% of our registered sport participants by the time they reach 15 years of age.

15. As things are, it seems without question that games and play are for the skilled few rather than for the majority.

16. When adults begin structuring play and games for all children, the issue of youth play, games and sport will cease to be a problem.

17. When children make up or create games for other children, there are three noticeable trends: A) children do not make up games where they eliminate each other from play; B) children do not make up games where they "hit" each other, and C) children do not make up games where they make other children wait in line to play.

18. Adults need to give the games back to the children.

19. Tell me what you play and I will tell you who you are.

GAME TEACHING – THE EFFECTIVE TECHNIQUES

Want to be successful leading games and activities? Read and practice these thirteen effective leading techniques. Most often when games or activities do not "play" the way you envision them to "play out", it was likely that the leader or leaders did not practice or were unaware of one or more of the techniques listed and explained below. If you take the time to read, learn and practice all thirteen of these techniques, you will have much more success...... I promise!

There are thirteen factors that influence successful and effective game leading. These factors can and often do vary in importance from game to game. There is no one technique that stands out among the rest nor is there a technique that shouldn't be practiced. It cannot be stated strong enough that a firm understanding and regard for these techniques can enhance effective game teaching ability.

Effective Game Leading Techniques

Techniques	Explanation
KNOW THE GAME	Don't be fooled by the apparent simplicity of a game. Be familiar with the rules and details. The best way to be familiar with a game is to play it and to play it more than once. It is obvious to the players when a game leader does not know the game or has not played it.
KNOW THE TYPE AND SIZE OF THE PLAY AREA	Structure the play area so that it will be fun and safe. Do not take up "game" time by having to measure boundaries or play space. Stop the game to change the size of the play space if it will improve the "flow" of the game.
HAVE A POSITIVE AND ENTHUSIASTIC ATTITUDE	People want to have fun and they like to play. Take charge of the game and show enthusiasm. Throw your energy into the game. It will make everyone else want to play harder and longer.
ORGANIZE THE GROUP	Get the group into the formation (a circle, two lines, etc) before stating the rules. Give clear commands, "When I say "GO", I want everyone to form a circle around me.""Ready, GO". If it's necessary to pick teams, divide them quickly using a creative method.
HAVE THE EQUIPMENT READY AND IN PLAYABLE SHAPE	Make sure there is adequate equipment for all players or groups. It may be necessary to check over a game site before playing or to arrive early. Do not come up short. It is not fair to the players and is reflective on the leader.
GIVE BRIEF INTRODUCTIONS	The game should start as quickly as possible. Do not give elaborate instructions. Questions can be answered during the demonstration. It is often best to speak less than to speak too much.
ALWAYS DEMONSTRATE THE GAME	Remember to talk less and demonstrate more. The game should be demonstrated until the players have a basic understanding of the game. Make it clear that the demonstration does not count as being part of the game (for scoring, etc). It may be necessary to demonstrate a game in slow motion, or one part at a time. This is a good time to answer questions.
PROJECT YOUR VOICE	Position yourself so all of the players can see and hear you. Do not stand in the center of a circle. Encourage players to speak up when they have a question. Use a visible sign to get attention or to get the group to be quiet (hold a fist high in the air). Use your voice to keep control.
ESTABLISH THE RULES, DON'T TELL THE PLAYERS HOT TO PLAY THE GAME	If you violate this technique, you will deprive the players of the very reasons for playing, i.e. individual discovery and problem solving. Be aware that some games play best with certain age levels or with specified numbers of players or with specialized equipment. Tell players the rules and how to play, not what they will experience.
CHANGE THE RULES IF NECESSARY	Play games that work. Be aware of IT POWER. The purpose of play is to establish an environment that is fun and comfortable for all players. If a game is not working, stop the action and change or alter elements of the activity to increase game flow. Always remember to play safely and to make sure players use the "Stop Play" command when necessary.
PLAY THE GAME YOURSELF	Become a player in the game if safety is not as issue, but never relinquish voice control. Re-introduce yourself as the leader if a problem arises. Playing the game gives you a better feel for what the players are experiencing and allows a basis for improving some aspects of the game. Besides, it's more fun to play.
END A GAME NEAR ITS HIGHEST POINT OF EXCITEMENT	Remember the lessons of game flow and the proper use of IT POWER. Let the players know how much time will be spent playing a particular game or when a game will be over. In the case of games with scoring, this will allow adequate time for players to get to a peak or to plan one more opportunity to score. Learning to identify when a game peaks takes practice.

IT POWER

IT POWER is the power of the individual or collective IT in a game to accomplish the goal, i.e. to tag players, to find someone, to guess correctly, etc. That power might be very high, very low or somewhere in between. The amount of power in any particular game is influenced separately by both the skill of the player(s) and the structural elements of the game i.e., what are the rules, familiarity of the game, how big are the boundaries, etc.

A significant number of games in this book contain IT POWER to some degree. Therefore, the ability to understand and apply this concept is central to the development of a leadership style for the effective teaching of games. Good games are not enough. After all, games are for players and players are different. Hopefully, the purpose behind the clean, fun game is for everyone to play well. For this to happen, it is necessary to keep the proper balance between the challenges in the game and the possibilities for success for both the IT and the other players. This can be done by modifying the power of the IT.

Whenever the IT is struggling or having difficulty because they can't catch anyone or guess anything, it's likely that other players are not having much fun either. The IT may be anxious because of the difficulty of the task, while the rest of the participants are bored because it's so easy. This is where an understanding of both the player's needs and the factors influencing IT POWER can go a long way toward providing more fun and can be used to facilitate a successful play experience.

Let's look at some of the factors that influence the IT POWER of the game and see how games and activities might be modified to increase fun and success.

Nine Factors that Influence the Power of the IT

Factor	Explanation
SIZE OF THE PLAYING FIELD	As the playing field gets smaller, the power of the IT to accomplish a task increases. As the playing field gets larger, the power of the participants' increases and the IT is challenged at a higher level. Balance is the key.
MODE OF LOCOMOTION	If the IT had to hop on one foot while all of the other players could run, mobility and thus power of the IT would decrease while the power of the players to avoid being tagged or caught would increase. There are many modes of locomotion (skipping, hopping, walking fast or backward, etc.)
THE POSITION OF THE IT	At the start of the game, the IT can be in the middle of the field (medium power), near the line of players (high power) or with their back to the players (low power).
STARTING SIGNALS	The game can begin when the IT says "1, 2, 3," or at random, or on a delayed start. Consider starting players by the first letter of their first or last name. Each varies the power of the IT to confront the other players.
POSITION OF THE PLAYERS	Players can all run at once from one goal area to another or they can run from two, three or four different directions. Each different player position influences the power of the IT.
THE IT'S TAGGING OPTIONS	The IT can use a variety of methods for tagging players. If an IT is having difficulty tagging players in a game, the Leader may give the IT a ball to throw at players. Once the IT tags a player, that player may have to rotate in a circle before tagging back. This would increase the power of the IT to accomplish the task of the game.
EQUIPMENT	The type and amount of equipment available to the IT will affect the flow of the game. If an IT has only one ball to accomplish a task, adding additional balls will increase the IT's power. Consider size of ball, how far a ball can travel or using objects other than balls (bean bags, balloons, etc)
THE NUMBER OF THROWERS/TAGGERS	In a game involving throwing, increasing or decreasing the number of throwers will affect the IT's power and the activity of the other players.
CUMULATIVE VS. REPLACEMENT ITS	In most tag games, the player touched by the IT is becomes the new IT (Replacement). Another possibility is that players tagged by the IT become another IT, helping the first IT to tag players (Cumulative).

Change the games to fit the players. Games are not sacred. When adding to the IT POWER, remember, you're not cheating. You're starting the players from where they are, and attempting to arrive at solutions that the entire group of players can be comfortable with. It cannot be over emphasized that a key to successful game change is that your changes must work for the majority of the group.

Remember that the goal in changing games is to find a sense of balance, with no one group or individual perceived as having an unfair advantage. The principle of manipulating the factors that influence IT POWER to achieve a playful balance between challenge and success is applicable to almost all game forms.

Finally, perhaps one of the most crucial aspects of IT POWER manipulation is the creation of a safe space for the IT to quit, find a substitute IT, and be able to merge with the other players. IT POWER is a game method that works to create games that are fun, challenging and rewarding.

GENERAL GUIDELINES FOR PROCESSING AND DISCUSSING THE ACTIVITY WITH THE GROUP

At the conclusion of a game or activity, all of the participants and the leader should spend a few minutes discussing and analyzing what the group has experienced. Games are much more than fun and exercise. They can be tools to discover how we operate and react in the "real world" or in our daily lives. The leader or leaders and the participants have an opportunity after a "play" experience to talk about what just happened. These talks can be simple or very intense. It takes special training and experience to delve deeply into players' motivations, fears and actions during games. But, simple questions and observations by the leader and the participants can lead to improved quality of play and to more satisfying play conditions for all involved.

Guidelines for the Leader or Leaders

1. Try to suspend judgment and refrain from assuming player's motives.
2. Let players know what to expect.
3. Be clear about your role as leader: to ensure safety, instruct, facilitate, observe, raise issues, and clarify.
4. Be clear about where and when a player can have input and make choices.
5. Remember that timing and pacing are essential.
6. Help players turn negative feelings into positive learning experiences.
7. Remember: you can only take others as far as you have gone.
8. You can't expect to relate to the life experiences and problems of all individuals whom you work with.
9. Honest confrontations and open questioning are usually met with appreciation.
10. If the leader talks too much, the group will remain more silent and less responsive.
11. Setting up a one-on-one norm can stifle group interaction. Don't shut out participants.
12. Try not to over focus or get into unsolvable problems.
13. Look for common themes or issues in the group to link them to each other.
14. Be aware that many people may not be ready to deal with an issue the first time it is brought up.
15. A group many times reflects the problems or dynamics of its leader.
16. Learn to trust yourself and your intuition.

Group Processing Ground Rules for All Involved

1. The group should be arranged in a circle where everyone can see each other.
2. Try to keep the energy of the group within the circle.
3. Introduce the group process (include honest dialog, safety concerns, and constructive feedback).
4. What is spoken in the group will remain confidential among the group members.
5. One person speaks at a time without interrupting others.
6. Everyone in the group belongs in the group. Only the leader can change this rule.
7. Everyone is ultimately responsible for his or her own behavior.

Specific Topics and Questions to Consider for the Group to Discuss

Topic	Questions
THE GAME OR ACTIVITY	Tell me about the game. What happened? What do you think? What do you think about the activity? What was the purpose of the activity? What are your first impressions or feelings? What did you learn from the activity? Did you use any special skills during the activity? Would you play this activity again?
LEADERSHIP/FOLLOWER-SHIP	Who were the leaders? How were they selected? Did any of the followers want to be a leader? Did you meet the challenge?
PEER PRESSURE	Did you feel pressure (negative or positive)? Were there any conflicts? Did you feel that there was any sexism during the game? Were you able to share your feelings? Did anyone feel they were not listened to?
GROUP SUPPORT	How well did the group work together? How did the group come up with decisions or strategy? How did everyone interact? What can you do to improve the group interactions? Did you learn anything about others in your group? Was there any negativism during the game? How was it handled?
COMPETITION	Was competition necessary (self or teams)? Do you like competing? Does everybody? What could your group have done differently? What did you learn about yourselves? What part did you play in the activity?
SAFETY/SPOTTING/FEAR	Did you feel safe? Were you encouraged to play safely? What did you risk? Was there fear involved in this game? If fear was present, was it physical and psychological?
JOY/PLEASURE	Did you have fun and laugh during the game? Is this necessary? Compare your feelings before and after the activity? How could this activity be used in another situation?

METHODS TO PICK TEAMS OR PARTNERS

In order to create a safe and supportive play environment, it is important that game leaders use methods for forming groups and for partner selection that allow players to feel non-threatened and not left out. Choosing "captains" and "counting off by numbers" may have had their place in history, but they have no place in this book, nor should they be in anyone's book. I believe that choosing partners and getting into a group should be fun, creative and perhaps, a game all by itself. There is seldom a need for teams to be exactly equal in ability, especially in Cooperative and Cooperative Competitive game formats.

There are hundreds of "partner picking" or "team picking" possibilities. There is no one method that should be used all of the time as there is no one method that will work all of the time. Pick partners and groups by trial and error. Most of all don't be overly concerned about who teams or partners with whom. The result of a game is never as important as playing the game. To get you started in a positive direction, I have listed a number of ways for the leader to form teams and/or select partners. I encourage each leader, however, to invent their own.

Note: When using these methods, there will often be times when one team may end up with more members than another. It may be necessary to then further divide the largest group with another method or for the leader to select a few players randomly from the largest group and place them in the smaller group.

The best and quickest technique to use in combination with each method is to have some type of line available (painted line on a field or a line across a gym floor). Loudly state your method. Quickly then, have all of the players with one the same choice line up on one side of the line and all of the others on the other side of the line.

CREATIVE METHODS FOR SELECTING TEAMS OR PARTNERS

Raise your fist in the air. Hold up one or two fingers. People with one finger up, team one; people with two fingers up, team two.

Cross your arms. Left arm on top, team one; right arm on top, team two.

Count the letters in your last name. Five or less, team one; six or more, team two.

Close your eyes. Stand on your left or right foot. Right foot, team one; left foot, team two.

Interlock fingers and thumbs on both hands. Left thumb on top, team one; right thumb on top, team two.

Count off: Apples...Oranges; Cows..Ducks; Venus..Mars; Winter...Summer, etc.

Close your eyes. Open one eye. Left eye open, team one; right eye open, team two.

Whisper "Twinkle, Twinkle Little Star" or "Happy Birthday to You" in each player's ear. Have each player hum the appropriate tune and have all players find all of the other players humming the same tune.

A dream vacation. Camping and site-seeing in pristine wilderness or swimming and relaxing on a sandy beach.

Players from cities with more than 50,000 people in one group, players from cities or towns under 50,000 in the other group.

Pet dog or cat. All players who had or have pets, team one; no pets, team two.

Favorite dessert: Chocolate pudding and whipped cream or apple pie and ice cream?

The leader counts the number of players, divides by two, then commands all players to form two circles by linking pinkies.

Think about swimming. All players who have swam in an ocean, team one; never swam in an ocean, team two.

Long or painted fingernails verses trimmed or unpainted nails.

Month you were born. January through June, team one; July through December, team two.

Number of children in the family: oldest on one team, youngest on the other. Middle children divided by being next oldest or next youngest. Exact middle children are placed where needed.

Rock, paper, scissors. Close your eyes and make a paper or a scissors. Paper team one, Scissors team two.

Note: If it is important for teams to be "equal" in skill and numbers:

Quickly have all players locate another player of equal size (or height or ability). Then have them line up across from the partner on opposite sides of a straight line.

Have the players' line up in order of height, smallest to tallest. Then fold the line in half so that the tallest pairs with the shortest, the 2nd tallest with the 2nd shortest, etc.

LEARNING AND LEADING STRUCTURE

How do we learn when playing games and activities? There are three learning structures: 1) competitive; 2) cooperative, and 3) individualistic. When learning takes place, one of these structures or combinations of the three is utilized. Briefly then, when learning happens, that action may 1) obstruct the action of others; 2) promote the action of others, or 3) have no affect on the actions of others. In competitive learning, the success of one individual or team can be linked negatively to the success of other individual s or teams, i.e. "I have success if you or others do not have success". In cooperative learning, the success of one individual or team is linked positively with the success of other individuals or teams i.e. "I have success if you or others have success". In individualistic learning, the success of one individual or team is not linked positively or negatively to the success of others i.e. "I have success or lack of success regardless of other individuals or teams' success or lack of success".

What structure or structures do we use to lead games and activities? There are two proven methods,
1) as individual leaders and 2) as group leaders. The large majority of the time, the leader is an individual who is in a position of responsibility and a leader who practices effective leading techniques (page 117). The individualistic leader is usually the teacher, coach, parent, etc. To be effective, this leader must satisfy certain requirements.

EFFECTIVE INDIVIDUALS LEADING – Activities lead by an individual

Requirement – There must be present	Explanation
… an important and meaningful goal	This is usually the leading of the game or activity but it could be team building, self esteem development, etc.
… the perception of independent effort	The leader is on his or her own. No other assistance or reliance on another leader is necessary.
… the isolation of participants	The leader can lead almost any group independent of the relationship between the leader and the participants.
… clear accountability, procedures, and clarity of required skills	The leader needs to be organized, understand effective leading techniques and be ready to accomplish the goal.
…the availability of the necessary resources and materials	The leader needs to be prepared. Once the activity starts, the necessary equipment and structure must be present.

Cooperative leading is not utilized as often as individualistic leading but can be quite effective, especially when participants or peers lead each other under the direction and observation of an authority figure familiar with both learning paradigms. The games in this book have been prepared to be lead using both structures. The cooperative leaders are usually the participants, parents, students, etc. To be effective, these leaders must satisfy certain requirements.

EFFECTIVE INDIVIDUALS LEADING – Activities lead by a group

Requirement – There must be present	Explanation
… positive interdependence	The group must work together to effectively teach the game to the rest of the players.
… face-to-face promotive interaction	The group members must make decisions and help each other accomplish their roles and group goals. Individual group members must not "take over" leading the game.
… Individual accountability	Each group member receives key game information and also assumes a "role" during the teaching of the game. See Individual accountability below for specific roles.
… interpersonal and small group skills	The small groups of four or five must work together making decisions while allowing for individual autonomy.
… group processing	At the conclusion of the game or before leaving the play environment, the group should meet to discuss the process and outcome of their game leading experience.

Groups that effectively work together will approach the game/activity with a plan that has been worked out in advance. Group members will be supportive and helpful to one another and "pick up slack" if necessary. They will not dominate or diminish the role of other group members.

INDIVIDUAL ACCOUNTABILITY – EFFECTIVE COOPERATIVE (GROUP) INSTRUCTION

Traditionally, when games or activities are taught by a group, one or two of the group members take charge and dominate the instruction process. To assure individual accountability (one of the key components for effective group instruction), groups meet and agree upon a role for each individual that will be performed during the presentation of the game or activity. Groups then practice the game. Finally, the group presents the game to the other players.

Each individual in the group is assigned or agrees upon a role to be performed when the game is played. The four/five roles are:

ROLES FOR INDIVIDUAL ACCOUNTABILITY	
Group Organizer	This individual is responsible for getting the group into the formation that the players need to be in when the game starts. This may also involve using a creative method to select teams. The organizational pattern (located in each game matrix) will be helpful to accomplish this.
Group Instructor	This individual is responsible for providing a brief explanation of how the game is to be played. These instructions need to be clear and easy to understand. The cooperative group needs to discuss the game to help the instructor present the game rules.
Group Demonstrator	The demonstration is usually the most important task used to inform the players of how the game will be played. The individual responsible for demonstrating the game must precede slowly, answer questions and make sure that all players realize that the demonstration does not count. It may be necessary to demonstrate in slow motion.
Group Leader	This individual will be the leader when the game begins. He/she will give starting signals and necessary commands. Often, this person will also be a player relinquishing initial supervision but always ready to step back in to take control. The leader may stop the game to make changes (IT Power) and attempts to end the game at its high point
Group Processor	A fifth role for a member of a group will be to process and evaluate the activity at its conclusion. This role can be difficult. Processing provides a means to determine the success of the activity as an activity and as a tool to improve the quality of the experience for the participants. The entire Group may want to be involved in the processing.

TOURNAMENTS AND MOTIVATIONAL STRUCTURE

Some of the games in this book are competitive in nature. They "play" best using the competitive format. When considering competition, the thought of elimination surfaces. The type of elimination that a leader selects can vary but the end result usually is that one individual or team wins and all of the other individuals or teams lose. The author prefers cooperative competitive where there is an overall winner but emphasis is placed on team work and the fun of playing the game. To enhance the quality of the experience, the leader should consider different tournament formats. Each format offers unique opportunity for players or teams.

Entire books have been written about tournaments and tournament structure. The games in this book where a tournament is suggested have been prepared with most of the information necessary to run the tournament including brackets and the order in which the games should be played. But it is still necessary to provide more detail to game leaders who may wish to use other games in the book in a competitive format.

STEPS TO CONSIDER WHEN LEADING A GAME USING AN ELIMINATION TOURNAMENT	
Steps	**Comments**
Determine the number of players or teams	The names will be placed on a tournament board
Decide if you will be running a single elimination, double elimination, Mueller-Anderson or a Ladder	The type of tournament will impact the number of play opportunities each player or team gets
Determine the amount of time you have to establish and run the tournament	Allow time to pick teams, fill in brackets, discuss rules, assign roles (for assistance), etc.
Prepare brackets in advance or print once you determine the number of teams	There are many on-line sources to help you set up brackets based on your numbers
Place the names of players or teams on the brackets	Randomly place them where you want (director's decision) or consider seeding (if you understand it)
The brackets should be numbered in the order that the games will be played	Be sequential (G1, G2, G3) with the most important games played last
Start the tournament and move along as quickly as possible to avoid "sitting" around	The leader takes charge to run the tournament as efficiently and professionally as possible.
Continue the tournament until a winner has been decided	The leader can emphasize the importance of each game and minimize the final outcome

Helpful hints for running successful tournaments

1. Set up brackets using the power of 2: 2 brackets, 4 brackets, 8 brackets, 16 brackets, 32 brackets, etc. If the power of 2 cannot be met, establishing "Byes" may be necessary. This is more complicated and may require outside expertise.
2. Create the bracket before you meet your group. If you create a bracket for eight teams and 35 participants show up to play, divide up the players into teams of four and select three players to assist the leader (32 is an ideal number).
3. Seed only the top four teams. Place them on the brackets so that the top team will play the second best team in the championship game if both teams win their games.
4. Have all of the equipment, gear, markers, etc. ready to go.
5. Select a tournament format where all teams play more than once and consider a format where all teams or players play an equal number of games.
6. Know the rules and make sure the players know and understand the rules. Consider creating your own rules to keep the flow interesting and more fun for the participants.
7. Determine if you require an official who knows the rules and can settle disputes, answer questions during play, and measure points during games.
8. Set a time limit. This may be for each game or for the entire tournament.
9. Establish in advance a method to determine a winner in case of a tie.
10. Have fun. Announce the game and the scores as if it's the Super Bowl. Laugh!

FORMAT	ADVANTAGE	DISADVANTAGE	NUMBER OF GAMES
Single Elimination	Easy to run and understand. Lots of games can be played quickly.	Elimination may be too quick. Winning is primary emphasis.	N -1
Double Elimination	Every team plays at least two games. Participant interest is maintained.	Complicated because "new" games get added to losers bracket.	2(N-1) or 2(N-1) +1
Consolation	Lots of games can be played quickly. There is a winner of the losers.	The best team may not win. Who cares for a winner of the losers	N-1 (both brackets)
Mueller–Anderson	A continuous consolation playback. All teams play equal number of games.	May be humiliating to last place. Not enough emphasis on winning.	4 teams, 6 games 8 teams, 12 games
Round Robin	All teams play equal number of games. All teams play each other at least once.	Takes the most time to run. Requires more than one play area.	N(N-1) ÷ 2
Ladder	Winning is not a requirement. Emphasizes maximum participation.	Could appear complicated. Players must challenge each other.	Depends on how many challenges

Note: N= Number of players or teams.

SINGLE ELIMINATION

The greatest appeal of the Single Elimination format is its simplicity. It is easy to administer and to understand. Losers are eliminated, and winners advance to the next round until there is only one team or player left, the tournament winner. The Single Elimination format is valuable when the number of entries is very large, time is short, and the number of playing areas is limited. Of all the formats, this one requires the fewest games; however, half of the participants are eliminated after one game, and only one quarter of the participants remain after the second round. When more extensive participation is important and more playing areas and time are available, the use of this format is not advisable. It may be important that entries are seeded when using this format. See diagram below for a sample of an eight team Single Elimination including the sequence of when games should be played.

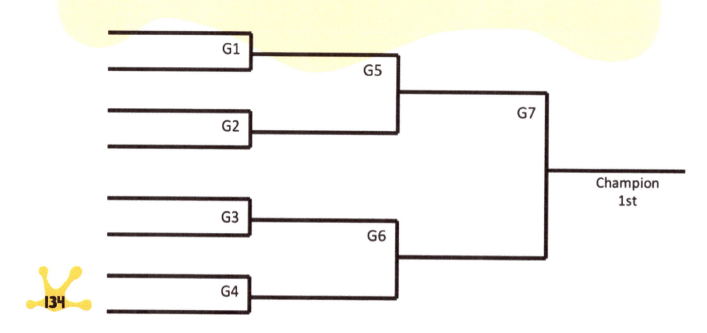

CONSOLATION ELIMINATION

The greatest appeal of the Conso-lation Elimination format is that all teams or players get to participate in at least two games. Losers are eliminated after the second round. The Consolation Format is valuable when there is a decided skill dis-crepancy because the winner of the Consolation bracket actually takes 5th place out of eight teams (or 9th place out of sixteen teams). In other words, less skilled players or teams have an opportunity to win a cham-pionship. Interest may sometimes be lost for the games played in the Consolation Bracket.

See diagram below for a sample of an eight team Consolation Elim-ination including the sequence of when games should be played.

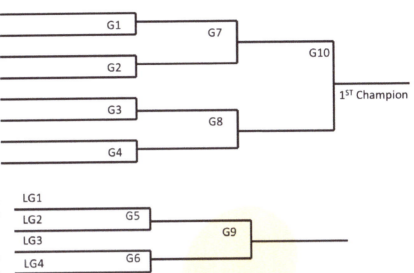

DOUBLE ELIMINATION

The Double Elimination format allows for teams or players who lose one game in any round of a tournament to get a second chance and to possibly win the entire tournament. When a team or players loses a game, they are placed in the "Losers" bracket and must keep winning or they will be eliminated. It may be important that entries are seeded so that the "best" play-ers or teams do not eliminate each other in the opening rounds. The winner from the winner's bracket and the winner of the loser's bracket play in the semi finals. "IF" the winner of the losers beats the winner of the winners, both have one loss and another game must be played (the "IF" game). The Double Elimination format can be confusing but usually maintains interest from all participants. See diagram below for a sample of an eight team Double Elimination including the sequence of when games should be played.

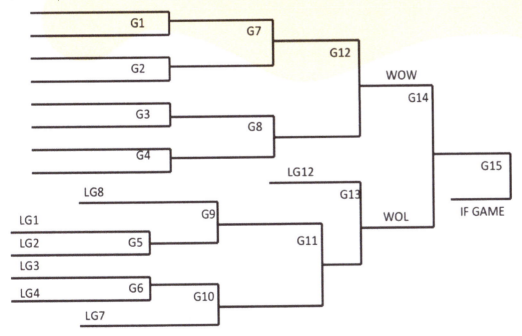

ROUND ROBIN

The Round Robin is a competitive format where everyone or every team in the tournament plays everyone else at least once, regardless of records. The player or team with the most wins is the champion. It is best used with ten or less teams or players. It is considered the best, most popular and most valid format to determine a champion.

One of the problems with the Round Robin format is that it can produce teams or players with the same number of wins. To determine a winner, a tie breaking method must be developed (in advance of the competition). The following tie breaking procedures may be applied: 1) use a scoring system (see table below); 2) the team or player that has defeated the other(s) will be ranked higher; 3)there can be a playoff, or 4) select a random method like a coin toss. Point differential should not be considered for recreation competitions.

ESTABLISH A SCORING SYSTEM						
Team or Player	Win	Lose	Tie	TOTALS		Points
Team A				W-	L- T-	
Team B				W-	L- T-	
Team C				W-	L- T-	
Team D				W-	L- T-	
Team E				W-	L- T-	

NOTE: One Win = 3 Points, One Tie= 1 Point, One Loss= 0 Points

After the number of teams or players has been determined, it is necessary to establish "rounds" or "rotations" so that everyone or every team in the tournament plays everyone else at least once. With an even number of teams or players (see example – Four Teams below), the first team or player remains stationary and the rest of the teams or players rotate counter clockwise for each round. With an odd number of teams or players (see example – Five Teams below), the Bye team or player remains stationary and the rest of the teams or players rotate counter clockwise for each round.

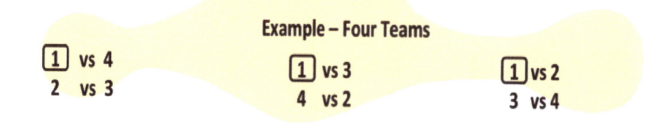

Example – Four Teams

1 vs 4		1 vs 3		1 vs 2
2 vs 3		4 vs 2		3 vs 4

Example – Five Teams

Bye vs 5	Bye vs 4	Bye vs 3	Bye vs 2	Bye vs 1
1 vs 4	5 vs 3	4 vs 2	3 vs 1	2 vs 5
2 vs 3	1 vs 2	5 vs 1	4 vs 5	3 vs 4

LADDER TOURNAMENT

In a ladder tournament, the ladder starts by listing members in roughly descending order of strength or at random. If the competitor with the lower rank beats the higher ranked player, he/she moves up the ladder to one spot above the player just defeated. If they lose, they stay where they are on the ladder. Individual events provide the most suitable activities for the ladder tournament format. The ladder tournament invites continuous competition and flexible scheduling. In a ladder, everyone remains in the tournament and stays motivated to continue climbing up the ladder.

The objective is to reach as high as possible on the ladder in a given time period. The lower ranked competitors challenge those with a better ranking. Players must accept challenges. Players may only challenge one, two, or three levels above their position on the ladder. There should be no "immediate" challenge backs. Players must play against another player before challenging a player that just beat them.

Many tournament formats lend themselves to blowouts and embarrassing losses. In a ladder, however, the best and worst players all experience parity. The lower ranked players challenge someone slightly higher on the ladder in order to move up in the rankings. This way, every player has an opportunity to improve his skill without getting embarrassed by an opposing player with a much higher level of skill.

| PLAYER OR TEAM A |
| PLAYER OR TEAM B |
| PLAYER OR TEAM C |
| PLAYER OR TEAM D |
| PLAYER OR TEAM E |
| PLAYER OR TEAM F |
| PLAYER OR TEAM G |
| PLAYER OR TEAM H |
| PLAYER OR TEAM I |
| PLAYER OR TEAM J |

CREATIVE GAME AND PLAY MATRIX

CREATIVE GAME AND PLAY MATRIX					
#	PLACE TO PLAY	EQUIPMENT	PURPOSE	MOVEMENT	ORGANIZATION	ENDING
1	Volleyball Court	Bean Bags	Learn Middle Names	Skipping	Sitting in a Circle	Magic Words Spoken
2	Gym Mats	Cones	Untie Shoes	Walk Backward	Toe to Toe	The # 10 is Reached
3	Basketball Court	Hula Hoops	Learn Birthdays	Side Shuffle	Tallest to Shortest	Everyone is Sitting
4	Grass or Carpet Area	Shoes	Everyone Gets Caught	Dance Step	Kneeling in Circle	The Music Stops
5	Side of Hill	Various Sized Balls	Create a Dance	Slow Motion	Scattered	Everyone has been IT
6	Under Mat or Blanket	Flags	Make Up a Story	Piggyback	Holding Hands	Everyone is Captured
7	Next to Wall	Toilet Paper	To Find a Partner	Baby Steps	Standing in Circle	All Know the Answer
8	Around Tree or Object	Rope/String	Play Without Talking	Marching	By Birthdays	The Light Goes ON/OFF
9	Playground/Open Space	Balloons	To End Up on One Team	Walk Stiff Legged	Partner-Locked Elbows	The Whistle or Bell Sounds

10	Around Chairs	Frisbees/Rings	To Make Funny Noises	Galloping	Linked Pinkies	Everyone has been a Leader
11	In Roped Area	Paper Bags	Recall Youth Memory	Hop/Skip/Jump	Back-to-Back	An Object is Found
12	In a Corner	Markers	Make Things Rhyme	Running	Lying Down	Everyone has a Turn to Play

CREATIVE GAME AND PLAY MATRIX – AN EXPLANATION

This matrix is a creative game teaching and playing technique based on the notion of forcing associations among and between game related elements. Six categories are identified and given specific information. A random selection of an element in each category results in a potential creative game experience. Individuals or groups of players undertake the challenge of cooperatively creating a game from the random information. The matrix presented to you offers the possibility of 2,985,984 different combinations of games. Each of the six categories contains twelve elements. To use the matrix, a number can be assigned to each of the twelve elements per category. An individual or a cooperative group selects a number (from one to twelve) for each of the categories. A number is selected six times (once for each category). These elements then become the specific information for a game to be created. See Appendix I (Page 139) for a larger Play Matrix.

Category	Explanation
PLACE TO PLAY	Twelve places that games may be played are presented. Once an area is selected or assigned, a game must be created using that play space. This play space may be real or imaginary. Dimensions, boundaries, type of surface, etc. and other considerations are left to the game designers. The place to play area that is selected can be used for the entire game or may be used only as part of the game. An attempt should be made , however, to incorporate this play area into the game format.
EQUIPMENT	Twelve different items of equipment are presented. Once an item is selected, the game must incorporate that item into the game either as primary or secondary equipment. Other items may be included by the game creators.
PURPOSE	Twelve different purposes or objectives are presented. Once a purpose is determined, the game creators must design a game utilizing this desired outcome.
MOVEMENT	Twelve different movements or movement patterns are presented. Once a specific movement is selected, a game must be created using that movement within the game process. This movement may be the primary movement within the game or may be used for only a small portion of the game.
ORGANIZATION	Twelve different organizational formations are presented. These formations indicate the pattern that is recommended for the players to be in to start the game.

APPENDIX A - DOODLE GAME SHEET

Name one thing that you can do really well.

What is your favorite memory of home?

If you could have any bumper sticker,
What would you say?

What is your favorite day dream?

APPENDIX B – FAMOUS PEOPLE GAME SHEET

First Name Letter	Last Name Letter	Full Name	5pts	10pts	25pts
A					
B					
C					
D					
E					
F					
G					
H					
I					
J					
K					
L					
M					
N					
O					
P					
Q					
R					
S					
T					
U					
V					
W					
X					
Y					
Z					
		TOTAL POINTS			

APPENDIX C – FANTASY GO-AROUND SHEET

FANTASY GO-AROUND

Each participant will decide on a personal "fantasy" that no one else playing this activity knows about. The "Fantasy" should be written with some depth or explanation. It should be possible. Example: "I have a fantasy that I would be able to live on a Caribbean Island in a grass hut with the love of my life. We would live off the land and be able to swim and fish in the ocean."

FANTASY GO-AROUND

Each participant will decide on a personal "fantasy" that no one else playing this activity knows about. The "Fantasy" should be written with some depth or explanation. It should be possible. Example: "I have a fantasy that I would be able to live on a Caribbean Island in a grass hut with the love of my life. We would live off the land and be able to swim and fish in the ocean."

FANTASY GO-AROUND

Each participant will decide on a personal "fantasy" that no one else playing this activity knows about. The "Fantasy" should be written with some depth or explanation. It should be possible. Example: "I have a fantasy that I would be able to live on a Caribbean Island in a grass hut with the love of my life. We would live off the land and be able to swim and fish in the ocean."

APPENDIX D – GROWTH CIRCLE SUGGESTIONS

STORY STARTERS	
I feel important when _____.	Something I never told anyone is _____.
My chores growing up were _____.	One time I got in "hot water" when _____.
My best surprise ever was _____.	The person who made an impression on me is _____.
I wanted to grow up to be a _____.	My favorite activities when I was in younger were ____.
I will never forget _____.	A secret that I wish I hadn't kept is _____.
I usually avoid _____.	Most people don't know that I _____.
My first job was _____.	The person that I most want to impress is _____.
I am happiest when _____.	My favorite movie of all time is _____.
I am most at peace when _____.	When I don't like people I _____.
I often crave _____.	The most difficult thing for me to do is _____.
My favorite book of all time is _____.	Other people see me as _____.
What I fear most is _____.	I was pushed out of my comfort zone when _____.
My biggest hope is that _____.	I would just really like to say _____.
I am superstitious about _____.	A place in the world that I would like to go is _____.
My favorite place is _____.	The historical moment I remember best is _____.
When I'm frustrated I usually _____.	Once I was really embarrassed when _____.
Life is _____.	I was named after _____ because _____.
I am secretly proud that I can _____.	The first thing that I ever remember is _____.
In five years I _____.	Something I hope people like about me is _____.
One time I got scared when _____.	I never thought that I could _____.
I always regret _____.	My favorite outdoor activity is _____.
Once I won a contest when _____.	The skill that I would like to master is _____.
My proudest moment was _____.	The most stupid thing that I ever did was _____.

ADD YOUR OWN STORY STARTERS	

APPENDIX E – MIME RHYMES LIST

KEY WORD	MIME WORDS					
tame	aim	game	came	dame	blame	lame
make	rake	bake	cake	fake	take	break
mare	wear	air	hair	bear	tear	scare
all	hall	ball	fall	wall	tall	mall
far	par	scar	tar	car	jar	bar
ash	dash	cash	smash	mash	bash	rash
farm	harm	charm	warm	arm	alarm	swarm
Bart	art	start	cart	part	heart	mart
hack	whack	back	sack	tack	pack	rack
hail	bale	fail	whale	tail	nail	mail
dang	gang	sang	bang	rang	hang	fang
mace	base	race	lace	pace	ace	face
mat	cat	bat	fat	hat	pat	rat
neat	heat	meat	beat	feet	seat	eat
lead	head	bed	red	shed	wed	dead
jell	hell	bell	sell	tell	well	fell
best	west	nest	test	pest	chest	rest
went	lent	tent	dent	sent	rent	bent
nil	fill	pill	will	kill	hill	bill
gig	wig	pig	rig	jig	dig	big
no	doe	blow	snow	toe	low	row
moat	vote	boat	float	coat	goat	wrote
ox	box	fox	socks	rocks	walks	pox
lug	rug	mug	hug	dug	tug	bug
bun	run	fun	none	ton	won	gun
hump	pump	bump	stump	jump	dump	rump
fee	key	bee	see	pea	we	knee
mutt	hut	gut	butt	rut	putt	nut
lie	sigh	die	cry	dry	tie	pie
tan	can	pan	man	fan	ran	van
gap	map	cap	rap	tap	nap	lap
rare	wear	pear	scare	chair	tear	hair
plane	grain	pain	chain	rain	mane	gain
clip	lip	flip	whip	dip	rip	sip
mod	sod	cod	nod	rod	god	pod
bold	gold	sold	hold	told	cold	fold
bum	come	hum	dumb	gum	rum	sum
cool	ghoul	fool	tool	stool	rule	pool
ream	cream	dream	seam	team	gleam	deem
keep	heap	creep	leap	peep	deep	weep
must	dust	lust	rust	bust	crust	gust
say	pay	way	day	hay	ray	gay
vern	turn	stern	urn	learn	fern	burn

APPENDIX F – NURSERY RHYME LIST

Jack and Jill went up the hill to fetch a pail of water, Jack fell down and broke his crown and Jill came tumbling after.	Old mother Hubbard went to the cupboard, to fetch her poor dog a bone, but when she got there the cupboard was bare and so the poor dog had none.
Georgie Porgie puddin' and pie kissed the girls and made them cry; when the boys came out to play, Georgie Porgie ran away.	Humpty Dumpty sat on a wall. Humpty Dumpty had a great fall. All the king's horses and all the king's men Couldn't put Humpty together again!
Hey diddle diddle, the cat and the fiddle, the cow jumped over the moon. The little dog laughed to see such fun, and the dish ran away with the spoon.	Peter, Peter, pumpkin eater, Had a wife and couldn't keep her; He put her in a pumpkin shell, and there he kept her very well.
Humpty Dumpty sat on a wall, Humpty Dumpty had a great fall. All the king's horses, and all the king's men couldn't put Humpty together again.	A diller, a dollar, a ten o'clock scholar! What makes you come so soon? You used to come at ten o'clock; Now you come at noon.
Higglety, pigglety, pop, the dog has eaten the mop; the pig's in a hurry, the cat's in a flurry higglety, pigglety, pop.	Tom, Tom, the piper's son, Stole a pig, and away did run! The pig was eat, and Tom was beat, And Tom went crying down the street.
Jack Sprat could eat no fat, His wife could eat no lean; And so betwixt the two of them, They licked the platter clean.	Oh, where, oh, where has my little dog gone? Oh, where, oh, where can he be? With his ears cut short and his tail cut long, Oh, where, oh, where can he be?
Little Bo-peep has lost her sheep and doesn't know where to find them, leave them alone and they'll come home, bringing their tails behind them.	Little Boy Blue come blow your horn, the sheep's in the meadow,cow's in the corn; but where is the boy who looks after the sheep? He's under a haystack fast asleep.
Little Jack Horner sat in the corner eating a Christmas pie, he put in his thumb and pulled out a plum and said "what a good boy am I."	Yankee Doodle came to town, A-ridin' on a pony; He stuck a feather in his hat And called it macaroni.
Little Miss Muffet sat on a tuffet eating her curds and whey Along came a spider, who sat down beside her and frightened Miss Muffet away.	Now I lay me down to sleep, I pray thee, Lord, my soul to keep. If I should die before I wake, I pray thee, Lord, my soul to take.
Mary, Mary, quite contrary, how does your garden grow? With silver bells and cockle shells and pretty maids all in a row.	Simple Simon met a pieman going to the fair; says Simple Simon to the pieman Let me taste your ware.
Old King Cole was a merry old soul, and a very old soul was he; he called for his pipe in the middle of the night and he called for his fiddlers three.	Rub-a-dub-dub three men in a tub and who do you think they be? The butcher, the baker, the candlestick maker, turn them out, knaves all three.

APPENDIX G – NURSERY RHYME MUSIC SCORE

Nursery Rhyme Song

APPENDIX H – *SIGNIN' IN THE SUN* MUSIC SCORE

Singin' In The Sun

(sung to the tune "Singin' In The Rain")

APPENDIX I – CREATIVE GAME AND PLAY MATRIX

CREATIVE GAME AND PLAY MATRIX					
#	PLACE TO PLAY	EQUIP-MENT	PURPOSE	MOVEMENT	ORGANIZA-TION	ENDING
1	Volleyball Court	Bean Bags	Learn Middle Names	Skipping	Sitting in a Circle	Magic Words Spoken
2	Gym Mats	Cones	Untie Shoes	Walk Backward	Toe to Toe	The # 10 is Reached
3	Basketball Court	Hula Hoops	Learn Birthdays	Side Shuffle	Tallest to Shortest	Everyone is Sitting
4	Grass or Carpet Area	Shoes	Everyone Gets Caught	Dance Step	Kneeling in Circle	The Music Stops
5	Side of Hill	Various Sized Balls	Create a Dance	Slow Motion	Scattered	Everyone has been IT
6	Under Mat or Blanket	Flags	Make Up a Story	Piggyback	Holding Hands	Everyone is Captured
7	Next to Wall	Toilet Paper	To Find a Partner	Baby Steps	Standing in Circle	All Know the Answer
8	Around Tree or Object	Rope/String	Play Without Talking	Marching	By Birthdays	The Light Goes ON/OFF
9	Playground/Open Space	Balloons	To End Up on One Team	Walk Stiff Legged	Partner-Locked Elbows	The Whistle or Bell Sounds
10	Around Chairs	Frisbees/Rings	To Make Funny Noises	Galloping	Linked Pinkies	Everyone has been a Leader
11	In Roped Area	Paper Bags	Recall Youth Memory	Hop/Skip/Jump	Back-to-Back	An Object is Found
12	In a Corner	Markers	Make Things Rhyme	Running	Lying Down	Everyone has a Turn to Play

APPENDIX J – NUMBER TO NUMBER DIAGRAM

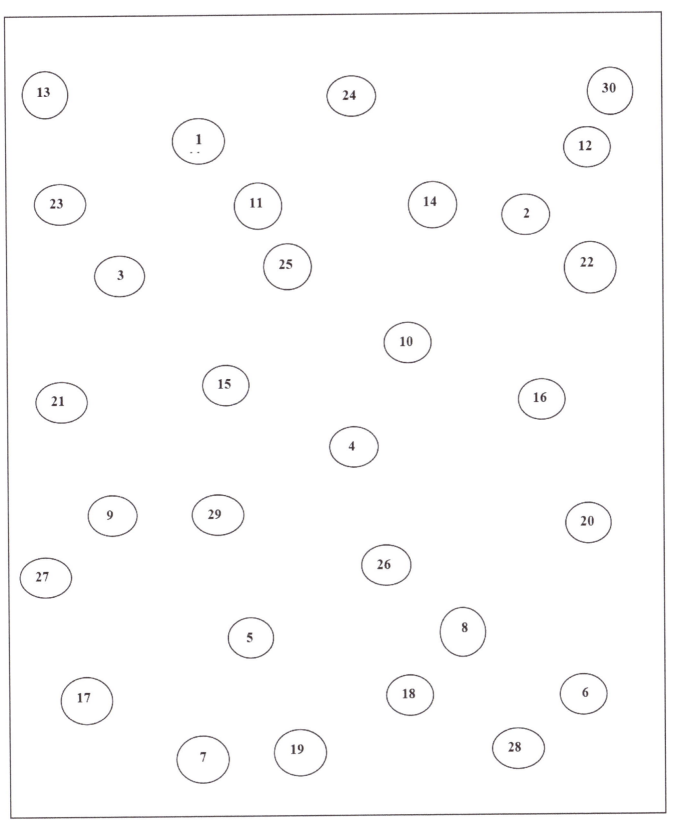

APPENDIX K – SOUND AND FURY COMMAND LIST

List of possible "FURYS" to accompany a player's "SOUND"

Jump on one foot three times!
Slap thighs five times!
Click your fingers twice!
Jump up and click heels!
Cross legs, sit down & stand up!
Do the twist!
Beat your chest like Tarzan!
Take a giant step forward!
Shake your body vigorously!
Throw a big kiss!
Clap your hands three times!
Turn around in a circle!
Salute with both hands!
Stomp foot three times!
Flap arms like wings!
Thumb on nose, shake fingers!
Do two jumping jacks!
Slap the top of your head twice!
Signal safe like umpire!
Shake players' hands next to you!

Swing a baseball bat!
Bend down , slap ground twice!
Do one push up!
Walk in small circles!
Point to the sky!
Whistle, two fingers in mouth!
Pretend to kick a football!
Jump on pogo stick!
Run three steps forward & return!
Dos-a-dos in a small circle!
Skip forward and back!
Lie on back and stand up!
Leap frog once!
Shadow box for three seconds!
Pull up both socks!
Lie on back and stand up!
Do a somersault!
Hands on ground and turn in a circle!
Crab position forward three feet!
Finger in cheek – make pop sound!

APPENDIX L – TOUCH AND GO COMMAND LIST

TOUCH AND GO COMMANDS	
TOUCH	**GO**
TOUCH something RED or BLUE or GREEN	RUN in Place
TOUCH someone's SHOE or SHIRT or HEAD	WALK around other players
TOUCH someone's EAR or HAIR or ELBOW	SPIN in a Circle
TOUCH a WATCH or MUSTACH or GLASSES	SKIP around the area
TOUCH the FLOOR or a WALL or a LINE	SIDE SHUFFLE to the LEFT or RIGHT
LINK Pinkies with eight players	MARCH forward
FORM a six person pyramid	Take BABY STEPS forward
PIGGY BACK ride on a players back	GALLOP like a horse
HOLD hands with four players	HOP, SKIP and JUMP
SIT down on a players knees	SLOW MOTION walk
LOCK arms while back to back with a player	DANCE to your favorite tune
PATTY CAKE with four players	WALK around backwards

APPENDIX M – PYRAMIDS DIAGRAMS

Pyramid #1

PYRAMIDS DIAGRAMS

Pyramid #2

PYRAMIDS DIAGRAMS

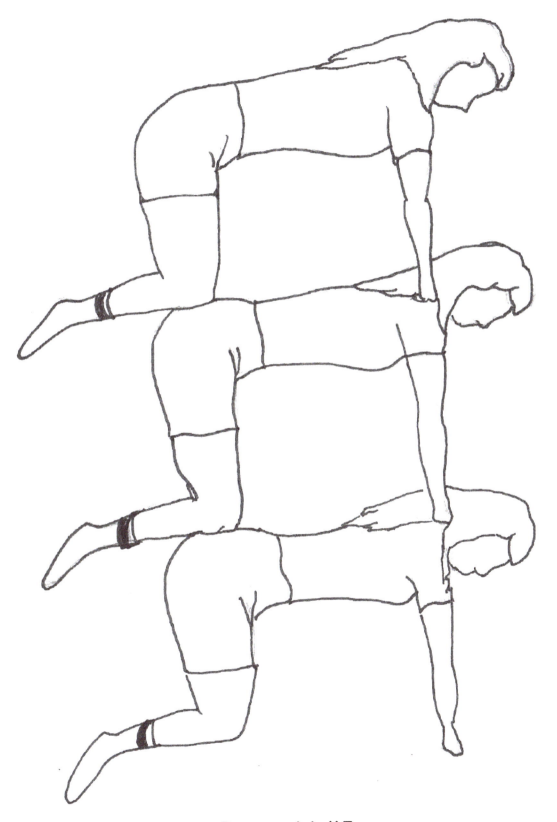

Pyramid #3

Pyramid #4

Pyramid #5

PYRAMIDS DIAGRAMS

Pyramid #6

PYRAMIDS DIAGRAMS

Pyramid #7

PYRAMIDS DIAGRAMS

Pyramid #8

PYRAMIDS DIAGRAMS

Pyramid #9

PYRAMIDS DIAGRAMS

Pyramid #10

Pyramid #11

PYRAMIDS DIAGRAMS

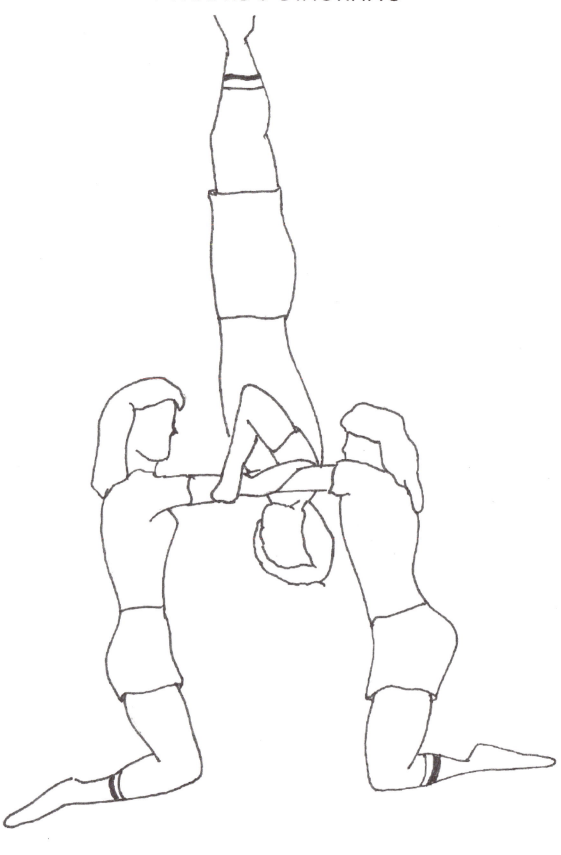

RESOURCE BOOKS AND GUIDES

Active Learning. by Bryant Gratty (Prentice-Hall). 1971.

Activity Program Fun. by Robert Steuck (Eddie Bowers Pub). 1983.

Bag of Tricks by Jane Sanborn (Search Publications). 1984.

Beyond Boredom and Anxiety: The Experience Of Play In Work And Games. by M. Csikszentmihalyi (San Francisco Press). 1975.

Circles of Learning: Cooperation In The Classroom by David and Roger Johnson (Interaction Book Company). 1986.

Cooperative Learning: Cooperation and Competition – Theory and Research by Johnson, Johnson and Smith (Interaction Book Company). 1989.

Cowtails & Cobras by Karl Rohnke (Project Adventure Press). 1989.

Effective Learning Goal Structure of Adult Learners During Non-Competitive Play by Michael Kinziger (Dissertation). 1992.

Essentials of Team Building by Daniel W. Midura and Donald R. Glover (Human Kinetics). 2005.

Every Kid Can Win by Terry Orlick and Cal Butterill (Pantheon). 1975.

Flow by Mihaly Csikszentmihalyi (Harper and Row). 1990.

Games! Games! Games! by George and Jeane Chipman (Shadow Mountain Press). 1983.

Games Teaching by E. Mauldron and H.B. Redfern (London, MacDonald and Evans). 1972.

Games We Should Play In School by Frank Aycox (Front Row Experience). 1976.

How To Change The Games Children Play by Don Morris (Burgess Publishing Company). 1976.

It Power: The Cooperative Game Experience by Michael Kinziger (unpublished Game Manual). 1992.

Joining Together – Group Theory and Group Skills by David and Frank Johnson (Allyn and Bacon). 1994.

Kids' Games by Phil Wiswell (Doubleday). 1987.
Learning Through Non-Competitive Activities and Play . Bill & Delores Michaelis. 1977.

More New Games by Andrew Fluegelman (Dolphin/Doubleday and Company). 1981.

New Games For The Whole Family by Dale Lefevre (Putnam Publishing Company). 1988.

No Contest: The Case Against Competition by Alfie Kohn (Houghton Mifflin Company). 1986.

Parachute Games by Todd Strong and Dale LeFevre (Human Knetics). 2006.

Playfair by M. Weinstein and J. Goodman (Impact Publishers). 1980.

Play With A Purpose by Dorthy Einon (Pantheon). 1985.

Processing the Adventure Experience by Reldan S. Nadler and John L. Luckner. (Kendall/Hunt Publishing). 1992

Project Learning Tree by American Forest Foundation. 2002.

Quicksilver: A Guide to Leadership, Initiative Problems, Adventure and Trust Activities by Karl Rohnke and Steve Butler (Kendall Hunt Publishing). 1995.

Raccoon Circles by Tom Smith (Raccoon Institute). 1996.

Silver Bullets by Karl Rohnke (Project Adventure). 1984.

Teamwork & Teamplay by Jim Cain and Barry Joliff (Kendall/Hunt Publishing). 1998.

The Bottomless Bag by Karl Rohnke (Kendall/Hunt Publishing). 1988.

The Bottomless Bag Again by Karl Rohnke (Kendall/Hunt Publishing). 1993.

The Cooperative Sports and Games Book - Challenge Without Competition by Terry Orlick (Pantheon Books). 1978.

The New Games Book by Andrew Fluegelman (Dolphin Books/Doubleday and Company). 1976.

The Second Cooperative Sports And Games Book by Terry Orlick (Pantheon). 1982.

The Well Played Game by Bernard DeKoven (Doubleday). 1978.

Winning Through Cooperation: Competitive Insanity, Cooperative Alternatives by Terry Orlick (Pantheon). 1977.

Cover lightbulb art designed by kreativkolors from freepik.com.

About the Author

Mike Kinziger resides in Deary, Idaho where he lives in a remote home in the foothills of The Rocky Mountains. He is retired from the University of Idaho where he taught and coordinated Outdoor Leadership for 17 years as an associate professor in recreation. Mike also taught recreation at the University of Wisconsin – La Crosse for 17 years as well as four years in a middle school. In total, Mike taught for 38 years accumulating seventeen teaching and outstanding performance awards. He has taught more than 25 different courses about recreational activities and creative play.

Since 1982, Mike has conducted more than 150 workshops and had speaking engagements across the United States directed toward team building and play in our lives. He also organized and directed a group called Just For Fun that provided recreational activity for special groups, corporations and school groups. Mike instructed at the International Clown Camp for five years where he taught clowns games that they could use when performing. He continues to conduct workshops and to speak at conferences.

Mike's outdoor experience includes everything from mountain biking to whitewater canoeing and he has led more than one hundred wilderness classes. He has been a scout, Vietnam veteran, athletic director and coached junior college basketball, tennis and golf. He is the holder of six long distance canoe records and is a role model for active, healthy lifestyle. Since retiring, he has completed five solo canoe adventures averaging three to five weeks in length in the Canadian wilderness. All of the trips were self-contained and involved no contact with other humans. His book on these excursions is called, "ALONE IN A CANOE".

Nick Cain earned a Bachelor of Science in Broadcasting and Digital Media at the University of Idaho. He began his career in Information Technology in Seattle working at a start-up. In 2017, he traded the mountains for the beach and moved to Atlanta, Georgia, where he now works in IT for a field management software company. In his spare time, he can be found enjoying outdoor activities like sand volleyball, cornhole, and Soccer. He also loves traveling, especially for music festivals, and going on adventures with his beautiful girlfriend and dog MJ.

Printed in the USA
CPSIA information can be obtained
at www.ICGtesting.com
LVHW061959170124
769035LV00056B/825